HAUNTED OBJECTS

Stories of Ghosts on Your Shelf

CHRISTOPHER BALZANO AND TIM WEISBERG

Published by

Krause Publications, a division of F+W Media, Inc.
700 East State Street • Iola, WI 54990-0001
715-445-2214 • 888-457-2873
www.krausebooks.com

To order books or other products call toll-free 1-800-258-0929
or visit us online at www.krausebooks.com.

ISBN-13: 978-1-4402-2991-6
ISBN-10: 1-4402-2991-0

Cover Design by Sharon Bartsch
Designed by Jana Tappa
Edited by Kristine Manty

Printed in USA

Acknowledgments

Special thanks go to those who chose to share these stories with us, and with the world, through this book.

Chris would like to thank: My amazingly understanding and supportive wife, Jill, and my two wonderful kids, Devin and Ella; Jeff Belanger for finding me another great project; the Spooky Crew for keeping my toe in the paranormal waters; my parents for pictures and support; and my students at Gateway Middle School for allowing me to use them as a sounding board for many of these stories. I would especially like to thank Tim Weisberg for stepping to the steering wheel with me and helping me bring these stories to light.

Tim would like to thank: my wife, Jennifer, my son, Adam, and the rest of my family; my fellow Spooky Crew members Matt Costa and Matt Moniz; the listeners of "Spooky Southcoast"; Jeff Belanger; and especially Christopher Balzano, who allowed me to get involved in this project and get my mind away from the need to prove the paranormal and back to just enjoying a good ghost story.

CONTENTS

6 | Introduction

16 | Section 1

The Ghosts You Wear

18: Stone's Dress | 23: Never a Bride | 24: The Little Girls' Dresses

28: Some Things Are Better Left Dead | 30: The Belt That May Have Started It All

36 | Section 2

Beware of What is Passed Down

38: Moving Moments | 44: What My Grandparents Left Behind: Tim's Story

50: The Mummy That Sunk the Unsinkable | 52: Uncle Webb's Tools

56: The Ghost of Two Christmases Past | 60: Three Ways to Get From Here to There

66 | Section 3

The Written Word

68: The Lady of the Lake | 73: Her Birth Certificate | 80: Knives and Shadow: Chris' Story

86: The Psychic, The Little Girl, and Three Killers

94 | Section 4

Ghosts at Play

96: The Haunted Violin | 100: Robert's Rules: Chris' Experience with the World's Most

Haunted Doll | 110: Claire the Doll | 116: My First Spirit Board: Chris' Story | 122: Sarah Finds a Board

126 | Section 5

Hauntings Around the House

128: Bed of Dread | 130: Altered Belief | 134: The Haunted Travel Clock

136: The Haunted Butter Dish | 138: Don't Sit There!

140 | Section 6

Haunted Jewelry

142: The Healing Medal | 144: An Assurance From the Unknown

148: I Dream of Djinn | 152: Rocks of Love | 153: Raphael on the Headstone

156 | Section 7

Off the Wall

158: Mirror, Mirror on the Wall | 166: Sacrifice | 168: Masking Evil

174: The Haunted Painting | 177: Poster Child

180 | Section 8

Wrapping Your Head—and Your Hands—Around Haunted Objects

182: Getting Attached | 185: Hands-On Experience

190: Haunted Collections | 194: I Bought My Ghost on eBay!

197 | Photo Credits

198 | Glossary

200 | Online Resources

202 | Index

207 | About the Authors

INTRODUCTION

Can an object be haunted? The answer is a resounding yes, and there are good reasons why.

O ur ideas of ghosts are formed by the stories we read or see on television. Sometimes they're molded by a personal experience we have.

Ghosts, or more accurately, ghost stories, are everywhere around us, but we do not understand as much as we might think about what a ghost truly is. We fall back on what we have seen on television or heard from others. In investigating ghosts and ghost stories, I've even found evidence that implies ghosts learn how to be ghosts based on what the person believed about the paranormal when they were still alive.

But can an object be haunted?

My story starts in the library.

Before the days of after-school child-care programs, I walked about half a mile to the local public library after class. I spent my time between the stacks, pulling out books and reading all types of tales until 5:30, when my mother picked me up. I read about dinosaurs and the universe and about countries in Asia I knew I might never see. There were two books I kept rereading, and looking back, it is not too much of a leap to see how they might have affected the rest of my life.

The first book was about how to be a private detective. It taught you how to sneak around the house, open doors without a sound, and interview suspects. The other was a collection of stories about unexplained happenings. One story featured a witch's grave where grass wouldn't grow, and one was about Daniel Webster fighting the devil on a cliff not too far from where I lived. There was also the story of a painting said to be haunted. It was of a castle with a light in one of the towers that would go on when odd things were happening in the house. If there was no ghostly activity, the window was black; if the ghost was around, the window was lit. There was even a time when a shadowy figure appeared in the window. In each instance, the paint-on window was dry. I was drawn into this story, and since then, my passion for all things unexplained has never left me.

Looking back, my analytical brain and my experience tell me this story has to be a piece of folklore. I accept there are things in this world I will never understand. Looking for ghosts and researching hauntings and folklore is often about discovering what can be possible based on scientific fact.

For example, people often say they feel a chill or a heat wave before something ghostly happens to them. Ghost hunters measure changes in temperature, believing the two are connected. The science makes some sense, but it can't be proven yet. I can handle that as a potential link, but dry paint that appears and disappears? It

Avoid dolls of any size or age, stay away from yard sales, and put anything you inherit in a safety deposit box.

spits in the face of every scientific fact and pseudoscientific paranormal fact—but that doesn't make the story a lie.

Years later, the story about the painting is one I still remember. It was not only the creepy nature of the tale, but also how normal the story started. It was just a picture. My father is an artist, and while I grew up, our walls were covered with framed bits of his creations. Could any of these lure a ghost? No one had died in our basement and I know the house wasn't built on an old cemetery. I was pretty safe. But those pictures … any of them could be a haunting waiting to happen.

If I only knew then what I know now. When asking if an object in your house is haunted, it is important to look at what we think we know about ghosts. The honest answer is very little. There are many theories out there, but some come to the surface more than others.

A spirit is the essence of a person or a moment in a person's life, somehow trapped in a way we can perceive. It might take the form of what we call a residual haunting—this means the essence is trapped, and lacking any consciousness, it acts like a recording of a moment or a person.

Think of it like this: A woman gets thrown down the stairs, screams, and dies when she hits the bottom step. Now, every night, at the time of her death, the residents of the house hear a scream and a series of pounds on the stairs and may even see the woman fall. She can't talk to them or move to a different room. They can't communicate with her. From a homeowner's perspective, all you can do is try to change the environment to break up the energy, or accept it and hope it runs out of juice. Keep in mind that some residual hauntings in Europe have lasted for centuries.

The other type of ghost is what investigators call an intelligent haunting. This has nothing to do with an actual IQ. It basically refers to a ghost with a mind that is still active and a "body" that can interact with its environment. It may be able to go from room to room, answer questions, and impact its surroundings in a variety of ways. The easiest way for ghosts to communicate is through electrical devices (see Uncle Webb's story on P. 52), but they are not bound by rules. They can move things, travel from room to room or off the property, and manifest in different ways. One day there might be

It's recommended to stay away from dolls and yard sales, and especially dolls at yard sales.

In many ways, it is almost logical that an object can be haunted, if you accept what we know about ghosts.

banging on the wall and the next day there might be an orb of light or a shadow in the room. It is difficult to predict what will happen next, although it is important to remember there are few cases in which people get hurt by ghosts.

There are many types of other paranormal elements that fall outside of these definitions. Poltergeists, which are generally associated with thrown objects and loud noises, may not be ghosts at all, but telekinetic energy from the living. Things like time slips, doppelgangers, and shadow people may not be ghosts, but often occur in connection with other unexplained phenomena in a specific location. Elementals, or spirits created by forces in nature instead of the remnants of living people, are ill defined but still blamed for turning on the faucet when no one is in the room. Then there are demons and dark forces that were never human and seem to have a sinister purpose for being in your house and may even try to possess you.

Silverware is among the common household items that can hold trapped energy, which can lead to a residual haunting.

All of this can be confusing, but it doesn't change the question: Can an object be haunted? The answer is a resounding yes, and there are good reasons why. In many ways, it is almost logical that an object can be haunted, if you accept what we know about ghosts.

A residual haunting—trapped energy—is more likely to be stored by an item near the event, especially if that item conducts electricity. It becomes almost like a character in the moment of the event. A crystal lamp or a setting of silverware becomes haunted and then replays the moment when the right environmental tumblers fall into place. The object can be moved to another location and when the situation is right, the recording replays, creating a haunting.

Intelligent spirits suffer from a bit of superstition, which may help to define why an item can be haunted. Many people believe ghosts can't pass on to the next world until all of their business is in order or they have resolved anything holding them back. Some may not even know they are dead. In these cases, they may use something familiar to hold, to communicate with, and will not rest until cherished items are in the hands of the people who deserve them. These may be objects that best defined the spirits in life, so it only makes sense the spirits can manipulate them in death. For example, a doll played with by a young girl who died is played with by an unseen force after her untimely death; a photograph of a mother is used to inform everyone she is okay; and an heirloom watch disappears when a son decides to sell it.

The trick is determining whether the item is haunted or just part of a haunting. We decided to chronicle both here, but only in those cases where a particular item stands out or seems to be the center of the activity. For example, there are few places with a richer documentation of paranormal activity than the Lizzie Borden Bed and Breakfast in Fall River, Massachusetts. We could have talked about the candlesticks that have flown off a shelf and hit people or written about the clock in the main room that runs slow or stops completely when other paranormal activity is going on. Instead, we chose the story of a misplaced book trying to communicate with a renegade psychic.

We should be straightforward about some of the choices we made in this book. The paranormal can be about evidence. In fact, seeing or hearing a ghost is what makes a haunting real for people and what makes paranormal TV shows so popular. But we have never allowed the lack of evidence to get in the way of telling a good story.

Many people believe ghosts can't rest until cherished items get into the hands of loved ones, which helps to explain why heirlooms, such as watches, can be associated with paranormal activity.

Some people have discovered common, household items they own are not what they should be and have become the focal point of a spirit.

We consider all the people who shared tales for this book to be reliable, and whenever possible, we try to back up their claims with evidence (the kind you find in a hall of records or a library). The stories they told are true to them and thus, that makes them true stories. You can't dismiss their feelings because you can't duplicate their experience.

Some people asked that we not use their real names or only use their first names, and we accommodate them. We present them to you, with our framing, of course, and allow you to make a decision on their truthfulness, if you choose.

This book contains true stories of haunted items and classic stories of possessed possessions, with an occasional urban legend and folktale thrown in. Don't worry, we'll tell you which is which, but sometimes that's not really important. A bit of truth lies in each folktale. Think of these stories as personal experiences mixed with superstition, the majority of which are told by everyday people who discovered something in their lives that was not what it should be.

Glasses, plates, and other pieces of china may look pretty harmless, and in most cases are, but sometimes these items can become a focal point of a spirit ... even a butter dish. Yes, really. See the story on P. 136.

Are the spooky noises you hear at night caused by something on your shelf? Maybe not, but then again ...

Most of the haunted objects are common, household items that, for one reason or another, became the focal point of a spirit. In almost every case, each object found its way into the hands of the people who reported the haunting. You're left wondering: Did the object choose the person, or did the person help the ghost make itself known?

That, of course, leads to the next question, one that might be harder to ask but will pass through your mind at least once as you read this book: Is there something on my shelf making those spooky noises I hear when I try to sleep? The answer is probably no.

The good thing about a book like this is that you can close it when the story is over and go back to the part of your life that believes ghosts aren't real. But then again, the people in these stories thought the same thing.

For now, turn to the first story, avoid dolls of any size or age, stay away from yard sales, and put anything you inherit in a safety deposit box.

— *Christopher Balzano*

Section One

THE GHOSTS YOU WEAR

Stone's Dress

One of the more intriguing aspects of any ghost sighting is what the apparition is wearing. Often the clothing helps us place the spirit, whether it is tracing it back to a certain person or to a specific time period. But what happens when the ghost leaves its clothes behind?

There is a long and haunted history at Stone's Public House in Ashland, Massachusetts. Captain John Stone built the structure in 1834, when he heard the railroad was going to run through his property. He operated it as a tavern and hotel for two years before leasing it to a succession of innkeepers. Over the ensuing 140 or so years, it fell into disrepair until Leonard "Cappy" Fournier purchased it in 1976. Once he began making renovations, the paranormal activity that had long been whispered about at Stone's increased tenfold.

The inn, known as the Railroad House during Stone's time, is believed to have been a stop on the Underground Railroad. It may also have a more sordid history. There have allegedly been at least seven deaths in the building. The footsteps of some of the victims are often heard echoing throughout the halls, and their spirits are known to move furniture. The first death involved Captain Stone himself, who murdered a man during a poker game and ordered him buried in the basement of the building.

Part of the dress found in the Stone attic.

One of the spirits associated with the location is that of a young girl, who can be seen staring out a second-floor window—a window to a storage room no living child is allowed to enter. Some believe she is the spirit of Mary J. Smith, killed on the train tracks outside Stone's in 1862 when she was just 10 years old. Although she was immediately brought into the Public House to receive medical treatment, she died shortly thereafter.

Even today, the staff reports hearing sounds of a young girl giggling or crying when there is not one present. There are also reports of the sound of a ball bouncing. But why would young Mary's ghost want to stay in the place where she met her grisly, untimely demise?

Her spirit is believed to be attached to the bloody dress she wore that fateful day, and it is allegedly that dress that resides in the attic of Stone's Public House. How it got there nobody knows, but no one wants to remove it—and for good reason.

The dress is ripped and tattered and stained with dark blotches that nearly everyone agrees appears to be blood. Over the years, it has become infamous among those wishing to check out the ghostly goings-on at Stone's Public House, but generally nobody—including the staff—is allowed into the attic.

That didn't stop one former waitress from sneaking up there and

Another piece of the mysterious dress.

taking the dress out. She took it home with her and was plagued by paranormal activity. She gave it to her boyfriend, who also had bad experiences while the dress was in his possession, even though it was locked in the trunk of his car. Finally, the waitress confessed to removing the dress from the building and returned it to the attic. Neither she nor her boyfriend had any more paranormal issues after that.

More recently, paranormal investigator Brian Harnois took the dress home while investigating Stone's for an episode of the Syfy Channel television show, *Ghost Hunters*, and also reported strange activity.

Independent paranormal researcher David Francis, who has worked closely with members of the Ashland Historical Society, first read an article about the bloody dress on the Internet years ago written by David Retalic, whom he said knows more about the ghosts at Stone's than anyone else. Intrigued by a haunted location so close to his own home, Francis began investigating Stone's and researching the history behind the haunting. The more he dug into it, the more he started to question whether the dress actually belonged to young Mary.

"I would have accepted this stance on the dress as fact, but as I began to explore the history of the Public House and its many legends, I started having my doubts," Francis said.

In April 2008, Francis and Retalic visited the attic. The dress was no longer hung

Mary's spirit is believed to be attached to the bloody dress she wore on the day of her grisly death, but no one wants it removed - and for good reason.

Whatever ghost is attached to the dress, she clearly doesn't want her clothing removed from its final resting place.

neatly as in past years; instead, it was in pieces that had been strewn about.

The first piece they found was a skirt made of pink, green, and white plaid. It had a velvet strip across the waistband with two metallic snaps. "It had occasional holes and stains littering the fabric in spots," Francis said. Next they found the top portion, a sleeveless blouse with delicate embroidery around the neckline and one button in the back to clasp it closed. The next two pieces they found were so worn, they were nothing more than rags.

"One piece was a large square of material with red and white stripes. In the white stripes was some type of floral screen print, and more of the dark blotches and stains were visible," Francis said. "The last piece was a long strip of heavy white material that had some sort of tie on one end. This piece had the largest stains of all the pieces, but their regularity on the piece seemed to suggest that the stains occurred after the item was folded into a smaller square."

Francis sent photos of the dress pieces to Linda White, owner of Linda White Antique Clothing in Upton, Massachusetts. White has been in business for almost 30 years, and her area of expertise is period clothing ranging from the 1830s to the 1970s.

White's belief was that the pinafore, sized for a child or young woman, was sewn on a sewing machine and was almost certainly from the Victorian era.

"The pinafore was in very good condition," Francis said. "A detailed report written by the Boston and Albany Railroad said that Mary was killed instantly after ignoring a flag man and running in front of the engine. If she had been wearing a pinafore at the time of her death, chances are incredibly remote that it would have made it through the ordeal so well-preserved."

White also said that the skirt itself could not have belonged to a young girl of 10, because the waist measured approximately 30 inches.

"She could also find no evidence of a waistband, and it appeared that the top section of the dress had been cut off to convert it into a crude skirt," Francis said. "And a close-up of the hooks that held the waist together revealed that the hooks and eyes were from the 1940s."

Francis, intrigued by White's analysis, eventually was able to bring her the actual remnants of the dress. White confirmed the original observations she made based on the pictures, but she was unable to identify the other pieces. However, she believes the grapes and swirls printed on the striped piece of fabric date it to the Art Nouveau period of the early 1900s, and that it is likely a remnant of a tablecloth.

"So we have two identifiable pieces, both from varying eras and belonging to two different women of different ages, and though we aren't sure just who the pieces belonged to, we can be almost 100 percent sure that they didn't belong to Mary Smith," Francis said.

If not Smith, then whom did these scraps of clothing with apparent blood stains actually belong to? Francis said they could have belonged to any number of people who stayed there during the many decades that the house offered lodging, including those traveling the rails, transient workers spending time in the area, and even prostitutes, although there is no concrete evidence to support that.

"There is reference to a 'cow yard' during John Stone's ownership, which is an old American euphemism for a brothel," Francis said. "Other than that, we have no concrete evidence to support the claim, other than the location of the hotel and its transient clientele offering a wonderful opportunity for any women who wanted to make some money in that capacity."

Although the actual owner of the dress may never be determined, it appears the garment has a spirit attached to it, nevertheless. It may not be Mary Smith, but whoever the ghost is, she clearly doesn't want her clothing removed from its final resting place in the attic of Stone's Public House.

Never a Bride

Just about every girl dreams of someday being a bride, of having that special wedding where she can be joined in matrimony to the man she loves.

But what happens when an overbearing father forbids his daughter to marry that man and ruins her perfect day? At the Baker Mansion in Altoona, Pennsylvania, it caused the wedding dress picked out for that ill-fated occasion to take on a life of its own.

Prominent local businessman Elias Baker owned the mansion at the time. According to legend, Baker's daughter, Anna, sought to marry one of her father's employees, but Baker refused to let her marry a common working man.

In truth, the wedding dress belonged to Elizabeth Bell, the daughter of another wealthy merchant in the area, who wore it on her wedding day in 1830. But as Maxwell Scott said in the film, *The Man Who Shot Liberty Valance*, "When the legend becomes fact, print the legend." So the dress has forever been associated with the forlorn lover Anna Baker. It is said she was so upset with her father that she never spoke to him again and never found love again, either.

When the Baker Mansion became the headquarters for the Blair County Historical Society, the dress was discovered and placed on display under glass. As the story goes, the dress began to move under its own power, swaying back and forth under the glass. The historical society volunteers blamed the movement on loose floorboards that caused the case to shake and the dress to flutter.

The dress is no longer on display because, according to rumor, it began to shake so violently it nearly shattered the glass case. The official line is that the dress was put away because the fabric was deteriorating. Those who believe in the undying nature of true love know the truth.

The dress is no longer on display because, according to rumor, it began to shake so violently it nearly shattered the glass case.

The Little Girl's Dresses

Sometimes ghosts can return in different forms to the same location. They may knock on doors, turn lights on and off, and even be seen from time to time. Some believe ghosts return to a familiar location to connect to the living world, perhaps to regain some sense of their own humanity. Are their loved ones still thinking about them? Are they still remembering them?

Others believe spirits never leave, that something traps them in a location; with an emotional anchor in place, they wander places that were once familiar to them until their energy dies or the location changes so dramatically it forces them to move on.

The house on Allen Street, where the two girls died.

There can be an emotional link between a ghost and an object, particularly if the ghost once owned it. This link was formed before the person died, and is the foundation of the idea of a haunted object.

Children, for some reason, are the one exception to that rule. Ghosts of children, who play with toys that do not belong to them and throw tantrums when they are taken away, plague many haunted locations. Investigators often bring toys to investigations as a means of making contact with children.

With all the hauntings in Chuck and Dodie's house on Allen Street, the dress in the upstairs guest room might have gone unnoticed. The property has seen much tragedy, and the night two little girls died in a house fire may have invited more spirits inside.

By the time Chuck and Dodie and their family moved in, the little girls had been dead for almost 20 years. During that time, people had moved in and out of the house, never staying long. The spirits of the young girls had been known to play with and steal tools from the men who worked on the property after the fire. A girl who lived next door always kept the shade pulled down in her room because she had seen the ghost girls across the yard too many times. The police officer who owned the house before Chuck and Dodie said he was selling it because of the strange activity there. Chuck and Dodie only had an odd sense something was wrong and misunderstood the sideways glances from friends who knew the house's history.

But there were more than the spirits of the girls in the house. Over the short time they lived there, Chuck and Dodie saw floating balls of light and dark figures, and objects disappeared and reappeared more times than they could count. The ghost girls were the most active, though. Their daughter's boyfriend spotted them on the landing of the third floor, where they died. They could be heard giggling when they pulled practical jokes, including turning lights on and off when male guests were taking showers.

The most lasting connection to the house took place in the room where the girls died. The newspapers had glossed over the details of their deaths, so as not to disturb readers, but unlike the quiet and painless deaths reported, the girls actually died of smoke inhalation, coughing and screaming before they passed out, according to bystander reports.

Immediate and prolonged suffering may be enough to leave something behind where it happened, and that seems to be the case on Allen Street.

Before they knew what happened on that night of the fire, Chuck and Dodie turned the room into a guest room. Dodie, who was interested in paranormal activity, didn't have a problem with the room at first.

"When we first moved into the house, I slept up there sometimes and found it a quiet, comfortable room," she said. Even after she found out what had happened there, she continued to use the room as storage, while still furnishing it with odds and ends.

"It was always hard to tell [if] what was happening [was] because of what piece of furniture [was there]," she said. "We had a great collection of what we called our Dead People Furniture. Whenever someone died, we got new furniture."

Dodie decided to hang some old dresses in the room for character.

"The dresses were handmade by Chuck's aunt for Chuck's sister," Dodie said. "She wore them as a child. There were two or three of them. When I had my daughter in 1986, his mom passed them on to her. I thought they were beautiful and hung them on hangers on the wall in a spare bedroom when we bought the house in Salem. Although all that was in the room was an air mattress and an old bureau, they looked cute hanging there."

The little ghost girls found ways to interrupt the everyday flow of the house and although they never did anything to threaten or upset the family, they seemed determined to make themselves known. Maybe because of their beauty or because they reminded them of dressing up, the dresses became the focus of the girls' activity.

"Everyday when I got home from work, I would make all the beds and pick up. No matter how many times I fixed the airbed in that room and puffed up the dresses, I would come back to find the bed a mess and the dresses smoothed down," Dodie said.

This ritual continued over time. Although the other things happening in the house were scaring them, the dresses remained just a sad reminder that not all moments from the other side are spooky.

"One day we were going out and I ran up to get a jacket. As I walked in

Of all the spirits that made the house their home, including some darker forces, the little girls never seemed to want to scare, as much as play.

the bedroom, I noticed the bed was a mess and the dresses smoothed down. I walked over and fluffed the dresses and turned to make the bed, muttering to myself because this crap was getting old fast," she said. "When I turned to get the jacket, I watched as the dresses were smoothed over right in from of me."

As Dodie fluffed them up again, she distinctly saw an impression large enough to be a person on the bed.

Until that moment, she had thought the activity almost funny. It always happened when she was not around and so she only saw the aftermath. But this was a bit too intense. While she wasn't scared, it proved too emotional for her.

Strain on the family, partly due to the hauntings, eventually made her leave the house and Chuck was forced to put it up for auction in 2009. By that time, he was no longer living in it, either.

"It was bought and redone. It's beautiful. From what I hear, the residents have been asking if the place was haunted," Dodie said.

Other family members continue to have experiences outside of the house, including ones so disturbing to Dodie that she brought in people to conduct a Native American blessing. Of all the things she experienced there, Dodie continues to return to the mystery of the dresses.

"There was never a feeling of fear surrounding the dresses, just aggravation that I liked them one way and an invisible hand liked them a different way. Chuck's aunt had passed by the time the dresses were handed down, so if it was her or the spirits that were already in the house when we moved in, I don't know. The dresses went back into storage, and I haven't heard anything more about them."

The little girls may have found something else to play with and perhaps they will someday be able to move on and find the kind of peace they once heard about in bedtime stories.

For her part, Dodie can only hope that the darker, scarier things in the house never interfere with the sweet souls of two lost girls who had the bad luck to get caught in a closed room during a fire. While living in the house, she saw dark spirits appear on computer screens, shadows float throughout the bedroom, and heard her children wake up screaming at things only they could see. Of all of the spirits that made that house their home, the little girls never seemed to want to scare as much as play or make themselves known. They may even still be there, hoping someone else will fill the closets with pretty new clothes to wear. Dress-up can still be a young girl's favorite game, even if she is no longer alive.

Maybe because of their beauty or because they reminded them of dressing up, the dresses became the focus of the girls' activity.

Some Things Are
Better Left Dead

Mary Ann and her husband were visiting an antiques shop not far from home one day when she spotted a faded pink parasol. It had a wooden handle and a tear in the material, with a yellow stain on one side of it. Mary Ann liked it, but the price tag said $60—far more than she wanted to spend.

Two weeks later, while perusing a local thrift shop with one of her friends, Mary Ann found what seemed to be the exact pink parasol. It, too, was faded, had a wooden handle, and had a tear with a yellow stain. Amazed, Mary Ann looked it over to be certain it was the same parasol. She wasn't going to leave it behind a second time, especially after she saw the price tag—just $5.

As she drove home with her friend, she remarked about how strange it was that the same parasol would go from an antiques shop to a thrift shop in only a matter of weeks, and then be sold for substantially less than it was priced just a short time before.

When she showed it to her husband, he agreed that it appeared to be the same parasol. They figured it was a stroke of good fortune that led Mary Ann to the parasol in the thrift shop. Perhaps, she thought, she was fated to own it.

She placed the parasol against their brick fireplace, the perfect spot to display her new treasure. Then she and her husband and friend continued on with their day.

Later, the three decided to go out for dinner. While they were upstairs changing their clothes, they heard a loud crash downstairs and ran to see what had happened.

The fireplace screen had tumbled to the floor. The fireplace tools, which had been tucked

They figured it was a stroke of good fortune that led Mary Ann to the parasol in the thrift shop. Perhaps, she thought, she was fated to own it.

inside the fireplace for the summer, were strewn over the floor, several feet away from the fireplace itself. The only thing left untouched was the pretty pink parasol.

Mary Ann's husband suggested maybe the cat caused the ruckus, but the animal was standing next to them, looking just as bewildered. It, too, had apparently been upstairs at the time of the crash.

They scratched their heads and began to wonder about that parasol. Perhaps the reason it had shown up in a thrift store at such a low price was because it was haunted. Whoever had purchased it from the antiques shop must have taken it home, had their own strange incident, and immediately donated it.

Mary Ann decided that was a good idea. She donated it back to the thrift shop—and the fireplace screen and tools never fell again.

The Belt That May Have Started It All

Researching haunted objects involves noting how things can be altered when such an object is present. Something is drawn to or kept in place by the item. Watching the way a spirit interacts with an object tells you something about both of them.

There are other times when a haunting is defined by something that is not there. In that case, the absence of an item that once proved to be a powerful symbol of someone's life can cause an imbalance. When that missing symbol has meaning for more than one person, when it may even be the connection many people have to a common history, it can spark something worse.

Most curses are active things, placed on people or places in times of vengeance or stress. They are invoked by the living, and they need to be nourished or they die. Many people think that believing in a curse might continue to give it energy even after the original person, who uttered the curse, has died.

The Wampanoag wampum belts fall somewhere between the two. There is no doubting their importance to a nearly wiped-out culture and their connection to a famously haunted area of the country. What we don't know is whether a spiritual explosion—which at times can be spooky and at other times downright dark—is part of an energy imbalance or is caused by a curse that remains active until the item in question finds its way back to the ones who revere it.

The reason doesn't really matter to those caught in the storm—they are just trying to understand what is happening to them and perhaps seek shelter from it.

New England is the heart of haunted America. With its architecture, long history, and dark and stormy nights, it has been the archetypal location for the ghost story since Nathaniel Hawthorn handed his mantle to people like H.P. Lovecraft and Stephen King.

In a corner of Massachusetts, right on the border with Rhode Island, lays an area known as the Bridgewater Triangle. Depending on which authority you listen to, the Triangle might stretch anywhere from the edges of Plymouth Rock all the way across the Nutmeg State. The highest concentration of paranormal activity in the country lies in this relatively small area.

Within the Triangle, anything is possible. It has been the home of UFO and Bigfoot sightings and the ground over which zombies are said to crawl. Ghosts are around every corner. Some towns embrace their haunted histories, while others

These Wampum belts at the Ripley's Believe It or Not Museum in Key West, Florida, are similar to those that were taken from Anawan.

wish everyone would stop talking about them. And while it may be the playground of supernatural creatures like giant thunderbirds and pukwudgies (troll-like demons), the area's high number of unusual murders, suicides, and cases of mental health disorders separate it from other places in the country that also experience ghostly phenomena. The Triangle has always been judged by the things that happen there, and the closer you look and the further back you go, the more you come to believe that the continuing activity is due to a lost belt.

The Wampanoag tribe met the Pilgrims when they first landed in this country, and at the time, they were the dominant people in the area. Although they had been hit by disease in the years leading up to the arrival of the Pilgrims, the Wampanoags' connection to other tribes throughout New England and their entrenched political and social systems made them a major force. Like most Native American tribes, they had no formal written language and passed on much of their belief system and history through the oral tradition. The map to their past and to who they were as a people was a series of wampum belts worn by the sachem, or leader, of the tribe. Although there is no visual record of what these belts looked like, research has uncovered certain details.

According to anthropologist and author Charles Robinson, the belts would have been about nine inches wide and could have wrapped around an average-

Most curses are active things, placed on people or places in times of vengeance or stress. They are invoked by the living, and they need to be nourished or they die.

sized man several times. Each belt would have consisted of shells and other natural elements, some worn through years of use. The most common colors may have been black and white, but similar belts from other tribes featured red, gray, and purple as well, with significance added to the color, shape, and size of each new shell that was added.

During ceremonies, the sachem would tell the history and important moments of the tribe, noting the shells that related to those moments, like a person taking out the items of a time capsule and telling our modern history through them. It was the job of the younger generation to listen and learn and eventually pass the stories on to the next generation. Until they learned to read and write, this was how the Wampanoag's history was recorded. By the time they began to record the stories in writing, they had already been influenced by the religious and social ideas of the European settlers who had converted them.

The wampum belt, which had passed through many hands in the preceding years, was lost, and the true history of the Wampanoag was lost along with it.

In 1675, war broke out between the people of Plymouth Colony and the Wampanoag, with most of the tribes in the area choosing sides. King Philip's War all but destroyed the Native American presence in New England. There are many causes of the war, and some might say the conflict was inevitable as soon as people crossed the Atlantic Ocean, but there are two definite things you can say about that dark year in America's history. The first is that the bloody nature of the war reflects the worst in human nature. The second is that the wampum belts, which had passed through many hands in the preceding years, were lost, and the true history of the Wampanoag was lost along with them.

Massasoit, the sachem in charge when the Pilgrims landed, passed the wampum belt to his son, Alexander, upon his death. In turn, Alexander passed it on to his brother, Philip, who wore the belt through the beginning days of the war named after him. As the fate of the war seemed certain, Phillip gave the belt to his general, Anawan, for safekeeping. Philip's visions held true for he was betrayed by one of his confidants and killed. Anawan, knowing ultimate defeat was near, surrendered in August 1676 and was stripped of the belt. Whatever became of it after that is unknown.

In his book, *True New England Mysteries: Ghosts, Crimes, and Oddities*, Robinson offers some possible locations for the belt based on his research. He records that General Benjamin Church did receive the belt and shipped it to England. He also found references to the belt in letters to and from England, but not proof it ever arrived.

Perhaps it was lost at sea or never cataloged when it was unpacked. Or perhaps the authorities had no desire to log all the treasures of war that passed across their desks. What is clear is that few people across the pond would have understood the significance of the belt, and even fewer would have appreciated it. Despite efforts in recent years to confirm its location in England, the belt remains lost.

It would remain just a footnote, a historical mystery, if the oddities in the Bridgewater Triangle—the site of so many emotional high points of the war and the heart of Wampanoag culture today—didn't have so many connected hauntings.

On Route 44, considered by some to be a type of paranormal artery running through the Triangle, a lasting tribute to the Plymouth betrayal draws in locals and paranormal investigators alike. The site of Anawan's surrender and the place where he was stripped of his belt is one of the most notorious places people go to look for ghosts. In fact, people not looking for ghosts often find them there as well. People have heard voices chanting and yelling in what has been translated to be Algonquin Indian. Small fires that give off no heat or sound appear and disappear. Even phantom Wampanoag warriors roam, often ready to fight when they come across visitors.

Profile Rock, part of the Freetown State Forest, also has its share of spectral sightings. Some written sources say Anawan received the belt from Philip at

Anawan Rock, site of the final betrayal.

The Triangle will continue to be a source of unexplained paranormal activity, as well as a magnet for darker elements, until a balance is restored.

that spot, and then stayed there to try to contact his father in the spirit world. Philip's ghost has been seen on the rock. Witnesses who have seen a man sitting there with his legs crossed say he vanishes when they approach. A few have seen a translucent man standing with his arms outstretched.

The list goes on: A disturbed burial site causes all the workers who discovered it to relive battles from the King Philip's War; a couple who took a memento from another disturbed site were troubled when a ghost dressed like a Native American kept visiting them at night. Time after time, witnesses within the Triangle report running into spirits who they identify as Wampanoag. Some are brief encounters, while others last years.

A news article in 2004 reported that an unidentified Wampanoag spiritualist said the murder and violence in the Freetown State Forest, which has made it infamous on a national scale, would continue until the belt was returned. It was the first time anyone made such a claim on the record. In the years that followed, others have made the connection between the violence and the paranormal activity there. The tribe now uses the forest as a reservation, so it would make sense that any curse would be concentrated in the place they now call home.

Violence and the supernatural made the forest their home long before the tribe officially made it their center. It does not end with rumors, either. So many of the ghosts in that forest—and there are many that walk among the trees—are those of Native Americans who have died. Those souls might be trapped by the belt or its agents, but one thing is certain: The hauntings show little sign of stopping.

Mediums and people who talk to the dead tell a similar story. The Triangle will continue to be a source of unexplained paranormal activity, as well as a magnet for darker elements, until a balance is restored. Even some who do not know the history cite the belt specifically as the weight that can tip the scales back. Officials within the tribe keep quiet about their views of the paranormal significance of the belt. They support the efforts to return the belt as a means of restoring their history, not

Profile Rock, the haunted location where the belt was thought to exchange hands.

to make the ghosts go away. Either way, the spirits stay and make themselves known.

Both sides are looking for something different. People in the paranormal field are looking for a way to understand their relationship with the paranormal. For them, it is about the life they have now, as well as the life they may have later.

For the Wampanoag, the need is more basic. They know their past only through the eyes of the people who turned their backs on the old way. They spend time trying to retranslate a history they feel they only partly know, like trying to unravel a hand-knitted sweater stitch by stitch to make another one that looks almost the same. They do it through words now, not quite sure how to tell their tale in shells, and maybe even a bit scared that a record so fragile could once again be taken away.

Section Two

BEWARE OF WHAT IS PASSED DOWN

Moving Moments

The din of the graduation dinner fades away, as the father chimes on his wine glass. He says a few proud words about his son and takes out a shiny pocket watch and hands it to him. Both are beaming as he tells how he received it from his father, who inherited it from his father, as if most of the people in the crowd don't already to know the story. He comments on how the graduate is now a man, and the people erupt in applause. The watch will live for another generation.

If any items hold the soul of a person, even of a generation, they would be family heirlooms. They are automatic histories, not bought in a store or a pawn shop, but passed down through the family and teeming with the stories of that person's life—and often with the weight of several lives. It is not just about the age of the item. The object is meant to be a link to the past, often a trigger for stories about the dead, and it is the act of passing it down that may actually attach the spirit to it. When that heirloom is lost or abused, or the person owning it somehow needs to hear about his or her heritage, something is triggered.

There is the story of a man who was known to crush rattlesnakes with his favorite pair of boots. One day the man dies of what seems like snakebite symptoms. His son inherits the boots, but not his father's silliness. A few weeks later, he dies in the same way, and there are some whispers about the sins of the father. The boots find their way into the deceased son's closet until his own son turns 16. He slips them on, remembering how much he loved his grandfather and father. He's dead soon after, another apparent victim of the curse. But when the boots are examined after the funeral, an old rattlesnake fang sticking through the sole is found, with enough venom left on it to kill 10 men.

The story is a legend, but it points to some of the ideas behind things passed down. They can be a gateway to a time long ago, but they can also be a prison, a mistake waiting to happen again and again. In some cases, they even offer a way to release a dead relative from his or her own sadness.

Pictures are a way for us to connect to our past, even if that past is one we didn't know

Pictures are a way for us to connect to our past, even if that past is one we didn't know we had.

The camera that was handed down from grandfather to grandson.

we had. Today everyone has a digital camera; most people even have one on their cell phones, making them within easy reach at any given time. But we are only a couple of generations removed from the time when a camera was a cherished item few people owned and even fewer mastered. Pictures were taken carefully using a different ritual than we use today, and it was after the "click" that the real work began. Owning a camera often meant having to develop the film yourself, and the intimacy with the process brought about a different love for what was captured. The pictures were transferred to slides and shown with pride. When the first moving film cameras came out, the emotional stakes were raised. You could immortalize those important moments of your life with motion. More importantly, you could pass it down.

Eli remembers having to sit through his grandfather's slide shows, although he remembers more how he tried to stay awake as his beaming grandfather would stop at every picture and tell a story about the moment. "It's not that his stories were boring, but I guess they were," Eli said. "I had just seen them my whole life. I loved my grandfather, but he had a way of thinking the most uninteresting things were exciting. He never really lived outside of the area he grew up in, so a trip to upstate New York was like going to Paris."

By the time he owned his own video camera, weighing about 10 pounds and needing to be carried on his shoulder, Eli had forgotten about most of the home movies he had seen, although he remembers the process of his grandfather taking out the projector and rolling down the screen on days when he would have rather been outside playing.

"'This is history, Eli,' he used to say. 'Your history.'" He fondly remembers staying at their house, but it took him years to realize why his sisters and cousins never went through the same ritual. As the only male, his grandfather must have seen him as the family historian, the person who was responsible for passing down their traditions and their stories.

When Eli returned home from work that night, the camera was on the bed. "I moved it back and made a comment to the air about Grandpa not touching my things," Eli said.

His grandfather passed away when Eli was 30 years old and lived five states away. His grandmother had died many years earlier. His uncle, who cared for the old fellow, was the one who called Eli with the news. "It tore me up, but you knew it was coming. I never had a chance to say goodbye, or at least didn't before he died. I think that didn't sit right with him. He had to try and find a way to come back and give me one more lesson," Eli said.

It began the night he heard his grandfather was gone. Eli spent most of the day getting things in order so he could leave to attend the wake and funeral. He was worn out when he finally fell into a heap on the living room couch. That night he dreamed his grandfather was in the room, sitting in the chair next to where he lay sleeping. He was tapping him on the shoulder, trying to wake him up, and when Eli finally opened his eyes, his grandfather was smiling at him and trying to talk. No sound came from his lips, but he was eagerly chatting, moving his hands around excitedly.

When he arrived at his grandfather's house, he was greeted warmly by his uncle. "I remember thinking how he didn't seem broken up at all," Eli said. "This was a guy who had already made peace with his father's death. I wasn't quite there yet." He was more surprised that the first thing he asked Eli to do was follow him into the basement. He showed him an old cardboard box and said his grandfather was adamant in his final days that Eli must have the box.

Inside was an unorganized collection of slides and 8mm films in canisters. Buried underneath were an old-fashioned film projector and film editor and a Sankyo Super LXL 250 camera used for taking film pictures. "The thing weighed at least five pounds and ran on two AA batteries. It must have cost a fortune when it first came out, but it still ran, although I was unsure where I could get film for it," Eli said.

After the funeral, Eli brought the box back to his apartment and placed it in the basement, where he was assigned a locked storage shelving unit. He kept the camera in his bedroom because he liked the antique feel of it. "I just thought it was cool," Eli said. "There's this old camera, and he had left it to me. I didn't think much about it, but everyone commented on it. To me it was only a conversation piece. I loved my grandfather very much, but I just didn't get into the whole picture thing. It was nice having a piece of him around, but I had no intentions of being the family documentarian or anything. I had some rocky times with my folks. Nothing too bad. I was just me, and the last thing I wanted was to be the head of anything. My grandfather had other plans, though."

The film editor.

About two months after he died, Eli's grandfather's birthday arrived. It was a sad day for Eli because it forced him to think about his deceased loved one again, and he was surprised at how many of the old slide stories he remembered. It was not the details of the pictures but his grandfather's sharing of them that remained. When he returned home from work that night, the camera was on the bed. He thought nothing of it, since he shared his apartment with several other men who frequently entered each other's rooms looking for books or CDs. "I moved it back and made a comment to the air about Grandpa not touching my things."

That night he had a vivid dream he could not explain. A younger version of his grandfather was walking down the stairs of his house. He was pointing to an American flag hanging from a pole in the yard and walked across the lawn to where Eli's father, who was maybe 10 or 11, held a sparkler. His father began running down the driveway and the vision shook and then went black. He woke up and turned the light on. "I remember thinking I had just seen one of my grandfather's old movies and when I turned the lights on, the camera was on the floor again," he said.

The dream had an impact, especially because it seemed his grandfather was trying to communicate with him. He dressed for work, vowing to not tell anyone in his family because he thought it would upset them too much. When he got home later that night, the camera was again on the bed.

When he got home later that night, the camera was again on the bed.

"I knew my grandfather was making all of this happen, and he was a man who would never hurt me. That didn't stop me from being scared at what was going on. I was always into ghosts. I just didn't want it in my bedroom."

"I asked my roommates if they had touched it, and they looked at me kind of weird. One said he had seen it on the coffee table earlier in the day, but he hadn't moved it because he thought I was trying to get it to work."

Eli placed it back on his shelf, but when he went to sleep that night, he had another dream. In this one, his grandmother was entering the kitchen with a lit birthday cake. His father was seated next to his uncle, who was about seven. He was jumping up and down in his seat and clapping his hands and the camera shook again as he blew out the candles. Eli saw a hand appear from off camera and give the thumbs up. Then everything went black. His room was fully lit when he woke up, and in the middle of the room was the camera again.

"I was pretty freaked out by now. I knew my grandfather was making all of this happen, and he was a man who would never hurt me. That didn't stop me from being scared at what was going on. I was always into ghosts. I think something can remain on this side when someone passes. I just didn't want it in my bedroom."

He moved the camera back to the shelf and went to bed. The next morning he went down to the storage area before work. The lock was still on the shelf, but when he opened it up, two canisters were placed on top of the box like someone had taken them out of the box and moved them. He brought the canisters and box up to his apartment.

"The camera was floating in the room. It was pointed towards me, like someone was handing it to me. I could smell him in the room again, and then the camera dropped to the floor ..."

"I got out the old projector and hooked up the first reel. I remember I had my blinds shut and all of the lights off and was projecting it on the wall of my room. I knew what I was going to see, and there it was: my uncle's birthday party. The movie lasted maybe five minutes and then I watched my grandfather saluting the flag and chasing after my father on the second reel. I just sat there in my room, and it was like all of the air got sucked out of the room. I could smell his cologne in the room and just knew he was behind me."

The raw film.

When he turned around, the camera was again on his bed. Eli made a pact with himself that he would spend the weekend going through the films in the box and brought them back to the basement.

"That was not the right thing to do. That night it was like watching one of those propaganda films they show in movies. They were all of short scenes edited together with quick flashes. I saw my father getting married, a shot of some people gathering around a rosebush, me one Christmas morning jumping around with a Mickey Mouse guitar. I don't even remember them all. But the worst was when I woke up.

"The lights were all on again and the camera was floating in the room. It was pointed towards me, like someone was handing it to me. I could smell him in the room again, and then the camera dropped to the floor. I got right up and went down to get the box. The shelves were locked again, and the box was opened and the films were all scattered on the shelf. I put them all in and carried it back to my room," Eli said.

He knows he had watched all of the movies he saw in his dreams while his grandfather was alive because he remembered parts of them. For him, that does not explain how the camera moved or the fact he felt his grandfather so clearly in the room. The message was clear to him, though. He started a project transferring the film to VHS, and then more recently to DVD. That seemed to satisfy his grandfather's spirit for awhile.

"After that night, the dreams stopped and they haven't happened since. I have not made these pictures an obsession, but it has become a hobby for me to do this. I have even gotten a machine that allows me to take old slides and make digital pictures out of them. It hasn't stopped the camera though. When I go a few weeks without working on it, I'll come home and my camera will be on the bed. Now I just laugh and tell him I'll get back to my work as soon as possible."

My grandmother
always warned us
not to stay in the
pantry alone for too
long. She never told
us why, but we all
knew: That's where
the ghosts hid.

What My Grandparents Left Behind: Tim's Story

Perhaps if I'm going to share other people's experiences with haunted objects, I should share my own as well.

They say every person has one geographic spot that they consider to be their true center, the place where they really feel "home." Many of us spend our entire lives looking for that spot. I was lucky enough to have it from the moment I was born.

My mother's parents lived in a side-by-side duplex house in Randolph, Massachusetts, throughout my life. They didn't own it, but the people on the other side were their landlords and more like family than anything else. My mother and her three siblings had all grown up there and they swore it was haunted by a friendly spirit that lived in the third-floor attic, where the girls slept.

I had spent many nights there, especially when I was younger. My grandparents would take me every Friday so my parents could have a night out. I slept in a bed in my grandmother's room. I remember suffering from old hag syndrome—the feeling that something is pushing down on a person's chest (formerly believed to be the work of a witch, hence the name, but now believed to be the work of spirits or even demons) whenever I stayed there. I wouldn't wake up to the feeling, as most people do, but would instead awake to see the shadow of ugly claws forming on the wall over my bed and reaching for me. I'd brace myself for the impending pressure that would soon hold my body down, yet I was unable to scream.

In later years, I'd often spend weeks at a time at my grandparents' house during the summer. Growing up in a family of five children, it was nice to be the only kid sometimes. I'd spend my days helping my grandparents around the house and riding my bike all over town. At night, I'd sleep in a sleeping bag on the living room floor. I'd zip it up over my head because I knew I didn't want to see what went on during the night. I could hear footsteps up and down the stairs, which were just beyond the far wall of the room, and banging in the pantry off the side of the dining room, right next to the living room. My siblings, my cousins and I used to close each other up in that pantry for a scare, even though my grandmother always warned us not to stay in there alone for too long. She never told us why, but we all knew. That's where the ghosts hid.

My grandfather passed away when I was 19, and my grandmother followed a few years later. My Aunt Arlene lived with them and remained in the house after their deaths. I was planning a trip to see my aunt on one particular Saturday, and the night before I had an extremely vivid and lucid dream in which I was at the house, sitting at the dining room table and visiting with my grandmother just as I had when she was alive.

She crouched in the window, unsure of her next move, and felt two hands gently push her forward. Whatever spirit was there with her, it wanted her out before it was too late.

In the dream, we were discussing everything that was going on in my life at that time and she told me how proud she was of me. Neither one of us addressed the fact that she was supposed to be dead, but I remember feeling like it was the elephant in the room. Still, it was an extremely calming and serene incident, and it made me feel better about visiting the house for the first time since she passed.

Not long after that came the fire and with it the physical center of my universe was gone forever.

When the house burned down, the only person living on my grandparents' side of the duplex was my cousin Amy, who was just out of high school. She had originally moved in with Aunt Arlene, but our aunt was getting married and had moved in with her fiancé. Amy was sleeping in the third-floor attic, and the fire started in the living room of the first floor. Many years before, an extension cord had apparently been run across the room, under the carpet. It must have been worn down over the years, surged, and then sparks from the exposed wiring ignited the rug. The house was old and the walls and ceilings were paper-thin. It was probably fully ablaze in a matter of moments.

Amy woke up not by the sound of a smoke alarm, but by the feeling that something was wrong. She opened the door to the attic stairs; the flames were already licking the walls of the hallway. She was trapped. She ran to the window across the attic, looking down on the concrete walkway and the dirt driveway three stories below. There was nothing to break her fall, and the fall would probably break her.

She crouched in the window, unsure of her next move, and felt two hands gently push her forward. Whatever spirit was there with her, it wanted her out before it was too late. Amy hit the ground, shattering both her wrists, but otherwise unhurt.

My cousin was upset, however, when she remembered that a beloved necklace that was given to her by grandmother was left hanging in her attic bedroom. Because she was so distraught, my Uncle Tom decided to go into the house to see if he could locate his daughter's necklace. He thought it would be like finding the proverbial needle in a haystack, but when he climbed through the charred remains of the house to the third-floor attic—nearly falling through not one but two sets of stairs—there it was, hanging on its hook. Everything around it was charred and burned, but the necklace glistened as if somehow protected from damage by an unseen force.

At the time of the fire, I was in college and still living at home with my parents. I remember going with them to see the devastation the fire had caused, but I wasn't quite prepared for what I saw. All that remained was a crumbling pile of still-smoldering wood and plaster. All the happy memories I had of that place were forever tarnished by the image before me.

The fire department had boarded up the doors because it was unsafe for anyone to go in there, yet Uncle Tom had found a way in through my grandfather's basement workshop that had been dug out of the underside of the hill on which the house was built. In the back of the workshop was a staircase that led to the kitchen and the rest of the first floor of the house.

I remember my dad going up the staircase first and quickly coming back down again. He said the kitchen was too burnt, and he didn't recommend crossing to the dining and living rooms, where the destruction was even worse. Yet I still had to see for myself, so I climbed the stairs and opened the door to the kitchen.

Once it swung open, I saw the kitchen exactly the way it had always been when my grandmother cooked wonderful meals. I could almost taste the fried chicken, the aroma filling the air, and could see every last detail the way I'd always remembered it—from the pan of bacon grease atop the stove to the permanent coffee ring on the counter in front of my grandfather's coffee maker.

Then I shook my head and blinked my eyes, and saw the kitchen in its actual, truly horrific state.

Later on, while visiting Amy in the hospital, I shared that story with my parents. I often had discussions about ghosts with my mother's side of the family, but I'd never talked about them with my dad. He's a practical and rational guy, so I just assumed he'd brush it off and tell me there was no such thing. I was shocked when, in the parking garage of the hospital, he told my mother and me about what really happened when he went into the kitchen

Something else caught my eye ... an ugly pink flamingo. The heat from the fire had melted half of the plastic, making it look like a big pile of pink goo on a metal rod. On a whim, I shoved it in the car, too.

of the house. He heard a voice forcefully telling him to "get out," and he immediately complied. Nothing more was ever said about it.

Before I left the duplex for the last time, I wanted to take something with me as a token of remembrance from the house in which I'd essentially grown up. Nothing in my grandfather's workshop had been damaged by the fire, so it was a no-brainer for me to take his chair—a simple wooden chair that was probably part of some long-gone dining room set, or perhaps something he'd brought home from his job as a junk man.

He'd sit in that uncomfortable chair for hours at a time, stripping copper wire for cash and tending to his wood stove. I'd sit there by his side, watching him work, his hands hardened by nearly 80 years of life but still able to build nearly anything out of wood or spare parts. It was in that same workshop that he helped me launch my radio career at just 13 years old, wiring one of those old Radio Shack crystal kits.

As I was putting the chair in the back of my car, something else caught my eye. There, in a small flowerbed, was an ugly pink flamingo that had adorned the garden for as long as I could remember. Although everyone complained about this eyesore perched in the middle of all those beautiful flowers, my grandparents never got rid of it. The heat from the fire had melted half of the plastic, making it look like a big pile of pink goo on a metal rod. On a whim, I shoved it in the car, too.

When I got home, I took the chair and the flamingo into my basement bedroom. I had a little living area set up down there, too, with two couches, a coffee table, and an entertainment center. I put the chair in a corner near my air hockey table and weight bench and the flamingo up against the wall on the opposite side of the room. I then left, returning home around 1 a.m.

I crashed immediately after going into my room. Even though my bed was just a few feet away, I often slept on one of the couches because it was more comfortable. I dreamed of my grandparents' house as it was before the fire, but as the dream went on, panic set in. Soon the dream version of the house was in flames, and I was startled awake.

As my eyes opened, I saw my grandfather sitting in his chair across the room. It wasn't the first time a family member had seen his spirit—a few months after his death, during a family gathering on the front lawn, he appeared in the window of his second-floor bedroom. But this was the first time I saw his ghost, and I was a little frightened. He just looked at me; once our eyes met, he vanished.

The next night I was awakened in the middle of the night to see my grandfather sitting in his chair. Again, once he turned to look at me, he was gone. Finally, on the third straight night of his appearing in his chair, he didn't disappear immediately and instead pointed to the melted pink flamingo against the concrete wall.

I knew right away what he was trying to say: "Get that thing out of here!"

I didn't even wait until the next morning; I got right up and took it out into the back yard of the house. There were some woods behind the house, and I chucked the melted pink flamingo as far back there as I could. When I went back into my room, there was no sign of my grandfather in his chair, and he never returned to it again.

The remains of my grandparents' house were plowed over and another house rebuilt over it. The new house is essentially a modernized version of what was there before, and to this day, it pains me to look at it. It's just not right.

I'm not sure if the chair carried the spirit of my grandfather, or if it was attached to the flamingo. My gut tells me he'll always be sitting in his chair and that he didn't want any reminder of the fire, which is why he pointed to the flamingo. Maybe he knew I wouldn't want a reminder, either. Of course, all of this could have been avoided had he just thrown that flamingo away when we asked him.

On the third straight night of his appearing in his chair, he didn't disappear immediately and instead pointed to the melted pink flamingo. I knew right away what he was trying to say: "Get that thing out of here!"

The Mummy That Sunk the Unsinkable

Many feel the following story is nothing more than a myth, but if there's even the slightest bit of chance that it's actually true, it will go down as one of the most haunted—and deadly—objects in history.

According to legend, four wealthy Englishmen traveled to Egypt in the late 1890s or early 1900s to visit the site of a massive excavation. Hoping to collect some ancient Egyptian artifacts, which were all the rage among the English elite of the time, the four friends nearly fell over one another to purchase the prize of the excavation: the ornate sarcophagus containing the remains of the Princess of Amen-Ra, who had died nearly 2,500 years before.

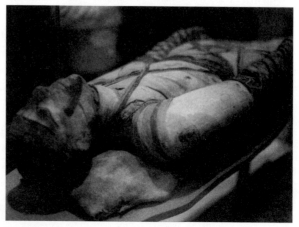

The mummy at the center of curses and tragedy.

Little did they know that the princess had placed a curse upon her tomb. The Englishman who purchased the sarcophagus wandered off into the desert, never to return. Each of the other three men also suffered great misfortune: One was shot by his servant and lost an arm, one went bankrupt immediately after returning from Egypt, and the other became terribly sick and lost his job.

It didn't stop with those four, either. The sarcophagus eventually made it to England and was purchased by another collector, who saw three family members injured in an accident and his house burn down before he finally realized what was causing all the bad luck. He donated the sarcophagus to the British Museum. While being unloaded, the truck it was on went into reverse, striking a bystander in the process. One of the men who carried it into the museum fell and broke his leg. The other died mysteriously two days later.

There are stories that a photographer took a picture of the sarcophagus and the image that resulted scared him so greatly, he shot himself that night, unable to shake the horrific image.

The sarcophagus was placed on display in the Egyptian Room, where more tragedy befell those who came near it. One night watchman died while on his rounds, and another quit because he couldn't take the banging sounds and muffled sobs that came from within it late at night. One person's child died of the measles, and other people who worked at the museum allegedly died after coming in contact with it. There are even stories that a photographer took a picture of the sarcophagus and the image that resulted scared him so greatly, he shot himself that night, unable to shake the horrific image from his mind's eye.

The museum knew it had to get rid of the cursed sarcophagus and sold it to a prominent American archeologist. It was to be shipped to New York aboard the state-of-the-art RMS *Titanic* in April 1912. Of course, it never made it there—it allegedly sunk to the bottom of the Atlantic along with 1,517 people who suffered its final wrath.

Legend has it the mummy may have caused the *Titanic* to sink.

Is that story really as unbelievable as it sounds? Many think it was the concoction of William Thomas Stead, a *Titanic* survivor who was also a journalist and ardent spiritualist. Stead allegedly made up the story in conjunction with another in which a medium warned him not to go on that fateful journey. There was never any record of such an item being loaded onto the ship, and surely something that valuable would have been logged and placed somewhere safe. And even the sarcophagus itself is something of a mystery; while many seek to explain away this curse by stating it still resides in the British Museum, the museum itself denies having ever had it in their possession.

Of course, nobody would want to admit to having something that caused so much destruction, pain, and death. So perhaps in this case, the old joke about denial "not just being a river in Egypt" applies.

Uncle Webb's Tools

Many people believe we need to find peace when we die before we can cross over to something eternal. After we pass, we want any problems we had to be solved, and for everyone to know how much we cared. Writing a will is a way to get that peace while we are still alive. Each person gets what he or she deserves, and the distribution of belongings is a way for us to assure our soul finds balance upon death. *Johnny gets the coin collection he always wanted. Susie gets the wedding dress, so I can be with her on her wedding day. Each grandchild gets money that will help him or her go to college.* All the pieces fall into place.

Unfortunately, that doesn't always happen, and the spirit can't move on until everything is right with the living. An object becomes the focus of a haunting. In this case, the spirit will continue hanging around, trying to communicate so people can understand. When that item remains a symbol of a strained relationship, the haunting might be even more intense. The need to get the object into the right hands becomes an obsession, sometimes for the living and the dead.

While everything on the surface was fine between Jimmy and his father, Webb, there was always something underneath that was unsettling.

Webb was always being confused with other relatives, so early on people suggested he drop his real name, Charlie, and go with his middle one. That suited him fine. There was uniqueness about the name "Webb" that made him stand out, and though many people considered him average, the people who knew him best said there was always something special about him.

"Uncle Webb was always the center of attention," said his nephew, Carl, who spent a lot of time with his uncle and cousins growing up. "If he was there, everyone else went to the background. Everyone wanted to hang with him. People just listened, like he was going to say something funny or deep. That guy made most things both at the same time."

Webb was a contractor who took great pride in his work. Coming from a blue-collar background, he wanted his son to follow in his footsteps and work with his hands and a

While everything on the surface was fine between Jimmy and his father, Webb, there was always something underneath that was unsettling.

Uncle Webb and Carl might have been close, but to the dead man, his unspoken intentions had not been followed.

Various tools.

good tool when he grew up. He told people about the business they would start together, working side by side, like he wished he could have done with his dad.

Jimmy wanted nothing to do with it. He went to college to become a teacher, and while his father eventually came to accept his career choice, he always took little jabs at his son.

"He wanted Jimmy to be a contractor, but to be honest, Jimmy was all thumbs. He couldn't even hang a picture," Carl said. Carl watched the relationship from the sidelines, listening to Jimmy when he talked about his father's disappointment in him. "I know it gnawed at Jim, but he got over it. It was like he was a teenager stomping his foot. He would pay people to do the easiest repair job, and find a way to slip it into conversation when we were all together. You could practically hear Uncle Webb biting his tongue."

In 2005, Uncle Webb died from cancer. He was still a young man with no thoughts of death and no will. He was not a rich man, so there wasn't a lot of money to distribute among the kids. Everyone assumed Jimmy would get his father's tools, as it is the kind of thing you pass down to your son, but Jimmy wanted nothing to do with them. Instead, they went to Carl, who had probably spent more time using them while Webb was alive than anyone else. He became a computer programmer, but understood the need to be useful around the house.

Carl's house, located a few miles from the mansions of Lakewood, Washington, has been a haven for ghosts since the day he and his family

"One night I was in bed and I heard a crash downstairs. I went into the basement, and all the tools were scattered around," Carl said.

moved in. For more than 10 years he and his wife and two children have shared the space with several different ghosts, although the house is much quieter now. For the most part, they have become used to the haunting and pass it off as part of their lives. They have never called in paranormal investigators or felt threatened.

"I did research, but nothing. No tragedy or little secrets," Carl said. "Just a house and a family that for some reason is a magnet for dead people."

The ghosts come and go, but the family can tell the difference between them by the activity in the house. Some move things around. Some run up and down the stairs. Little children are heard giggling at times. The most active spirit is that of a little girl they call Kay, who has a crush on Carl. While Carl dated the woman who is now his wife, Kay would lock the doors and pull the sheets off the couple. For years she would play with an old music box in the dining room, winding it up and moving it around the house. They even heard a humming along with the song. When their first child was born, they could not keep the baby out of the crib.

"I thought she might be jealous of the kids, but she protects them. I think it's kind of sweet. She's gotten used to my wife and just wants to play. I have no trouble with her now," Carl said.

The little girl's spirit has become a part of the family, but it's the spirit of a different family member that has caused the most disruption. Uncle Webb, who probably would have fallen in love with the house when he was alive, had issues with the family. He and Carl might have been close, but to the dead man, his unspoken intentions had not been followed.

"It started two weeks after the funeral," Carl said. "I had set up a little work area in the basement and put all the tools down there. One night I was in bed, tired after a long day in front of a [computer] monitor, and I heard a crash downstairs. I went into the basement, and all the tools were scattered around. I know I hung all those tools up and organized everything down there."

He did not get around to putting the tools away until that weekend. When he observed the mess that Saturday morning, he noticed none of the hooks that held the tools were bent, and the tools were thrown about the basement in places they could not have naturally gotten to. "A hammer was under an old desk I have down there. For it to have gotten there, someone would have had to throw it. It's a good 10 feet away."

A few days later, Carl's wife noticed a picture had fallen off the wall. "It was on the kitchen table. I didn't put it there and my wife had nothing to do with it," Carl said. The glass over the picture, which is of his wife during a trip to Europe, was shattered. "There was a screwdriver right through the glass. It was like someone had tried to stab her in the picture."

His wife was frightened by the incident, even though the family had experience with the paranormal. "I know there are people in my house. This felt differently and we were trying to figure out who it might be," Carl said.

They got their answer in the next few days.

That picture had been in the attic in a box of pictures. There is no way it could have gotten into the basement.

"Uncle Webb had always liked the Beatles," Carl said. "Radios in our house started to turn on and play Beatles songs. We have a radio in just about every room in the house. They would turn on by themselves and a Beatles song would play. They'd be on stations neither of us even listens to. Three of them have to be hand-tuned, so it's not like someone hit the scan button or something. I began to wonder if it was Uncle Webb and what he wanted."

The couple decided Uncle Webb was trying to tell them that he had moved on. Tools continued to be moved and radios continued to play. After three weeks, they began to get tired of turning off radios.

"I asked him to tell me what was wrong. If he had something to say, I asked him to say it. I didn't really think I would get a response," Carl said.

That night, all of the radios in the house turned on, all playing the same song. Carl turned them all off one by one and moved to the basement to shut the last one off.

"There it was. All of the tools were in a perfect circle on the floor of the basement. In the middle was a picture of my cousin, Jimmy, and me. That picture had been in the attic in a box of pictures. There is no way it could have gotten into the basement.

"I figured he wanted Jimmy to have the tools. I packed them up the next day and drove to Seattle where he lives," Carl said. "I didn't tell him what happened. I just gave him the box and told him they belong to him. He was actually kind of happy about it. You have to put some things aside. Uncle Webb is dead, and I think Jimmy might think it's been too long. I'm not sure if he ever uses them, but they're his now."

Carl reports the music has stopped playing and the pictures now remain where they are hung in his house.

The Ghosts of Two Christmases Past

Every year, part of the Christmas tradition in the Balzano household is to decorate with some old family ornaments for sentimental reasons.

There is one my wife made in grade school and one my son made just a few years ago. One my father gave me goes near the top of the tree. We hang pictures of wreaths and candy canes our children made in grade school. Each has its own story that rings out across the years.

But what if an ornament could somehow store recollections of past Christmases? More importantly, what if those memories are not all that happy?

In the 1960s, Janet's mother purchased an ornament of a young girl wearing a Santa hat and sitting on a sleigh. It was not handmade or antique, just a simple clay statue.

Janet does not remember anything unusual about the ornament while she was growing up. When her mother passed away a few years ago, she inherited the ornament among other things. Eventually it made its way onto her tree and almost at once, there was something different about the holiday season. The rest of the house had a cozy Christmas feel, but the room where the tree was displayed had a heavy atmosphere and it felt like someone had died in it.

Janet began to hear banging, scraping, and the sound of ornaments being thrown to the floor at night. When she investigated, she found nothing.

Then came something else. When she was in the room where the ornament was, she heard a little girl crying. Living alone with no children, Janet knew the cries weren't coming from inside the room. The temperature also often dropped—

The ornament began to move. At first only to different places within the room, but then it began to move to different places within the house.

something paranormal investigators hear from people who experience ghosts.

Then the ornament began to move. At first it only moved to different places within the room, but then it began to move to different places within the house.

Janet eventually put the ornament in a box and moved it into the attic. She heard the cries several more times, but the activity stopped. She never displayed the ornament again, although she says that in the 30 Christmases that have passed since she packed it away, it's mysteriously reappeared on the shelf several times.

Another friend of mine had a similar experience with a set of Christmas angels. She placed the two white angels on a shelf, well out of reach of her three-year-old daughter, who had begun to talk about a little girl named Elizabeth who came to visit her.

Nothing unusual happened that first week the angels were displayed, but one day my friend saw that they had turned around and were facing the wall. She turned them back around and thought it was a joke played by her husband, who said the figures looked like they were staring at him.

> A red stain, like blood, was dripping down the wall right below the angels.

The next day the angels were again facing the wall. She turned them around and when her husband came home, she confronted him about it. He laughed it off, but her daughter overheard them and immediately offered a reason.

"Mommy, Elizabeth said the angels were naughty. They had to go into 'time out,' " she said. My friend told her daughter not to touch the angels again, although she noticed none of the chairs had been moved and her stool would have been too short to reach the shelf.

"I didn't do it. Elizabeth did," her daughter claimed.

The angels were facing the wall again later that night. My friend was certain her husband and daughter were not the culprits. She turned the angels back around and whispered, "Don't you move again," but later she saw they were facing each other.

Then other unusual things started to happen. The Ouija board they kept in the closet was found with its lid off. The lights flickered. Her daughter began spending more time alone in her room playing with her imaginary friend, and they were heard singing Christmas carols.

Before going to bed a few nights before Christmas Eve, she saw the

angels were again facing the wall. She picked them up, but then stopped.

"No," she said to herself. "I am ignoring you this time."

She went to bed but had trouble sleeping. When she went to check on the angels later, they were facing into the room. A red stain, like blood, was dripping down the wall right below them. She ran her finger over the stain and discovered that it was actually red candle wax. She searched her house the rest of the season for a red candle that could have made that mark, but was unable to ever find one. Nothing else happened that year, but she has not displayed those angels since then.

Three Ways to Get From Here to There

There is a saying that the whole is often greater than the sum of its parts. This does not always hold true for haunted items. It doesn't always take the whole to make the ghosts come out, and sometimes the displacement of parts can be what causes the imbalance.

There are stories of people removing an object from a sacred place, like a headstone

Some cars can carry a curse.

from a cemetery or a rock from a Native American ritual site, and the spirits follow the fragment home. It's as if you have broken off a piece of the whole and things aren't set right until it is returned.

Another type involves places like the Assonet Ledge in Freetown, Massachusetts. Known as a "body dump" for murderers and famous for its numerous suicides, it was a quarry until a lethal accident forced the business to close. In addition to the countless paranormal experiences people have had there, many buildings made from the stone are reported to be haunted as well.

In some cases, the whole is destroyed, but some of the parts continue to disturb people. People have blamed curses, bad luck, and spirits; others simply shake their heads and know it is only an urban legend. You're forced to ask questions whenever you hear a story like this, but the answers are never easy.

The Urban Legend

There may be nothing more American than our cars. From an early age, children, especially boys, are given toy cars to play with. Getting a driver's license becomes a rite of adulthood. Before we make an automotive purchase, we spend time choosing which car best reflects who we are—or who we want the world to think we are. Whether they are lemons or classics, we are connected to them. It's no wonder that so many ghostly experiences and spooky legends involve cars.

Perhaps the most bizarre of these is the cursed car, doomed to doom its owners through accidents and unusual experiences. There are two versions that have made the rounds most often, identical in theme, but different in the details. Here's a riddle: What does a Hollywood icon and a prince who threw the world into war have in common? Both took a wrong turn.

In his day, no person played the part of the rebel better than James Dean. In fact, he still exists in our modern times as

You never know if someone with haunted wheels will be on the road.

the man who lived the life people secretly want and fear at the same time. No one was cooler. For five years, he was the most wanted man in Hollywood. He embodied the idea of living fast, dying young, and leaving a good-looking corpse—until the day he did die and left behind nothing but a corpse and two legends. One legend involves the man himself and the stamp he put on our ideas of the young, troubled rogue; the other has to do with the way he died and the car that might have survived after he died.

It all supposedly started with a life lesson all people need to heed: *Listen to Obi-Wan Kenobi.*

As part of his fast-paced and dangerous reputation, Dean spent much of his time acquiring and racing fast cars. His favorite became a rare Porsche 550 Spyder he had customized and detailed to his specifications. In what would become a series of fateful moments, the car he originally wanted was delayed, and the Porsche was only supposed to be driven in the interim. It was nicknamed Little Bastard and according to sources, Alec Guinness (best known as Obi-Wan Kenobi in the original *Star Wars* trilogy) warned Dean a week before his death to get rid of the car or risk dying in it.

Seven days later, Dean was dead. On the afternoon of Sept. 30, 1955, shortly after being ticketed for speeding, James Dean collided head-on with a car going the other way on Route 446 in San Luis Obispo County, California. All others involved in the crash survived, but the legendary rebel expired before he reached the hospital. Since then, his image has appeared time and time again as an example of wasted youth and suave uncaring. Stories of that crash have grown as well.

The original rumors began with a common motif in urban legends: James Dean still alive but so disfigured by the accident he dare not show his face

Perhaps the most bizarre urban legend is the cursed car, doomed to doom its owners through accidents and unusual experiences.

When people look at its most infamous moment, they think the car might have had something to do with the death of more than nine million people.

and limit the potential earning power of his image. Similar things have been said about Elvis Presley, Tupac Shakur, and Heath Ledger, who, along with Dean, is on the short list of actors to receive an Academy Award nomination after his death.

The story that has persisted is more about the car, the murderous "Christine" of its time (some say the Little Bastard inspired Stephen King's tale of a killer car). It was salvaged by a used car dealer and used as a moneymaker and cautionary tale. According to Snopes.com and several other online sources, the vehicle was then bought by car customizer George Barris, whose mechanic suffered a severe injury as it was unloaded from the truck.

Barris allegedly stripped the car and sold off the parts. Troy McHenry and William Eschrid, two doctors living in the Beverley Hills area, got into an accident with each other immediately after using some of those parts to repair their own cars. McHenry died, as did another man who bought the tires from the doomed Spyder—they exploded the first time he took the car out.

Where are the car and its parts now? No one seems to know. One legend tells of it being transported by 18-wheeler to serve another stint as an example of how not to drive. On the way to its destination, the truck got into an accident, killing the driver, and the car was stolen. Another tells of it being transported but never arriving at its destination, even though the truck arrived late but in one piece.

Of course, none of this can be faithfully tracked to any reputable source. Barris spoke publicly about it, but was never able to have his version verified. Troy McHenry did die in a car accident, but in an actual car race, not racing a fellow doctor who also had parts from Dean's car. Instead, the circumstances of the crash and the legends of the cursed car feed one another, and while there may be no proof that either is true, they stand as an example that Hollywood stories are always made from a little bit of truth and a little bit of imagination.

The Confirmed Curse

Decades before Dean's crash, the hunt was already in full swing to reclaim another cursed car. This one was never as glamorous as Dean's car, but it saw more history than the Porsche. When some people look at its most infamous moment, they think the car might have had something to do with the death of more than nine million people. All this from a second-hand limousine, a questionable driver, and a curse no one can quite explain. Just like World War I was not "the war to end all wars," the car that sparked it continued to live past its prime.

The car was a 1911 open-topped Gräf & Stift Bois de Boulogne tourer owned by

Archduke Franz Ferdinand of Austria. Although he was the heir to the throne of the Austrian-Hungarian Empire, he had gained his titles and prestige more by accident and through family mishaps than through leadership and proving his worth. He married outside of his station (and was shunned by some of his own family for it), and seems to have played things close to the vest. This might have been one of the reasons he died on that fateful day in June 1914.

Ferdinand's country had annexed Bosnia, and while visiting there, several attempts were made on his life. Then on June 28, 1914, his new limo took center stage. A grenade was thrown at the car, but the device was poorly timed and ended up exploding behind the car. The Archduke and his wife drove on, eventually making a wrong turn. They were ambushed as they tried to back up and straighten out. A shot in the neck killed Ferdinand and forced Austria-Hungary to declare war. A short time later, ties and pacts threw most of the Western world into battle.

A wealthy doctor was crushed and another lost his clients and wealth because people were starting to whisper about the curse of the car.

The tourer was too nice to get rid of, so it continued to be driven during the war. General Oskar Potiorek, who was also in the limo the day Ferdinand was shot, inherited the car—but maybe he should have just bought a new one. He was beaten back in several battles by inferior troops, something outside of the highly decorated officer's usual modus operandi. He returned to Austria shamed and was stripped of his command. There are several stories of what happened to him upon his return, but according to Snopes.com, the most prevalent is that he lost his honor, money, and maybe even his sanity. He also lost the car, which went to his captain, who died a short time later: He killed two bystanders on a country road before hitting a tree and killing himself.

Again, the stories that followed the car in the next few years bounce between legend and fact. The next owner was known for getting into constant accidents with it until the last one resulted in his arm being amputated. A wealthy doctor was crushed and another lost his clients and wealth because people were starting to whisper about the curse of the car. Another man committed suicide in it. It then went on to kill a race car driver and a farmer before being retired to the Heeresgeschichtliches Museum in Vienna.

There are many ways to explain it. Bosnia, Serbia, and Yugoslavia, all places where the car killed, are not the safest places in the world, especially at the time the deaths took place. The poor quality of roads and the lack of driving skills back then could have contributed to the accidents as well. Not much is known about the drivers, either.

Some of the stories might have been confused over the years, especially in a place where the records are spotty from that time period. There's also something to be said for the power of a curse. Those who hear it tend to believe it and put themselves in situations where they are more likely to have bad things happen to them. In those cases, the curse takes on a life of its own.

What can be said is that people close to the car, at least those in the towns and cities where the owner lived, whispered how a single car might have been born to kill.

And the 'Real' Case

The case of Flight 401 might be the most well known and at the same time the least talked about tale of haunted items. People saw ghosts, but they spoke of them in hushed tones so they could keep their jobs. But what if some of their conversations were loud enough to be heard? What if government agencies confirmed their beliefs? You hear of people in the military talking about their experiences after they retire, but in the case of the people who crewed planes after the tragedy of Flight 401, the vow of silence has gotten stronger with time. In the coming years, the gags might come off, and maybe then we'll all understand the extent to which the energy from one source might fuel others.

The case has a solid, well-documented side to it. On Dec. 29, 1972, Eastern Airlines Flight 401 suffered what should have been a minor equipment malfunction and crashed into the Everglades of south Florida. More than 100 people died, most from the initial impact. The landscape was a blessing and a curse: It was more difficult to reach the survivors, but many lived because the thick mud and salty water kept infection at bay and helped with blood clotting. To many people looking at the accident from the outside, it was a wake-up call to the dangers of flying. But our country had become a nation of fliers by then, and people still took to the air for both business and pleasure.

The airplane business went on as well. Planes were well built with the best materials of the day. While it has never been fully released how much recycling went on, parts from the downed 401 were salvaged and used as replacement parts in other Eastern Airline planes. (Some parts from Flight 401 are still visible in the Everglades today.) Most were smaller, less vital pieces, but some say they still might have been big enough to store ghostly energy of the doomed flight. As parts passed from one plane to another, so did the spirits of the people who died that night. The accident caused ghosts to be seen in the skies for years.

The most frequently seen apparitions are those of two of the people who manned the plane. Pilot Bob Loft and flight engineer Don Repo were seen by dozens of witnesses in the years following the crash. Some people saw them in the windows or the mirrors of the plane. Others saw them among the people, sitting in empty seats or walking the aisles. There were even times when people interacted with them. While a few of the

The accident caused ghosts to be seen in the skies for years.

witnesses were people enjoying a flight, some of whom were later shown pictures and identified the two, others were people who knew them well and had worked with them. Some might say it was grief or suggestion, but people who had seen them in life were now seeing them in death.

One famous incident occurred when a flight attendant saw a face in one of the ovens while preparing meals. She called someone over to confirm what she as seeing, and the person happened to be a good friend of Repo's. He made a clear identification and was one of several people who heard the words, "Watch out for fire on this airplane." There was indeed a fire later on that flight, which forced the plane to miss one leg of its trip. Repo has been seen several other notable times as well. In one of the creepiest instances, he appeared to the pilot and told him everything was going to be okay. According to written testimony, he told the man, "There will never be another crash. We will not let it happen."

The initial reports were enough to warrant looking into, which of course led to books and movies. John Fuller published the most respected book on the subject in the mid-1970s, *The Ghost of Flight 401*, and other works followed. Then came the movies, and of course, the legends. None of these works, which sometimes tend to dramatize the paranormal aspects of the case, can take away the fact that an independent agency, the Flight Safety Foundation, found the stories and witnesses credible enough to issue a statement basically saying the planes might be haunted.

Eastern Airlines wanted nothing to do with the stories and forced people to remain quiet after the first batch came out. The airline always had a rocky existence, but things got worse after that. Eastern officially ended its run in early 1991 and has resisted attempts to get back into the air. For the paranormal world, this might be a good thing. In the waning days of the company, many people associated with it were laid off or fired, making for some disgruntled workers. After so much time has passed, people may be more willing to tell their stories, although many are no longer with us and took what happened to them to the grave. Paranormal researchers like Nancy Planeta are trying to track down people associated with the case to see if there are still stories left to be told.

What happened that night in Florida is the true definition of an accident. Mechanical error played alongside human error, and it cost people their lives. There is another side to the story, however. Those who saw the spirits of their old friends again must have lived the rest of their lives knowing something the rest of us don't, something that could not be forgotten with a gag order: some part of us exists after we die.

Section Three

THE WRITTEN WORD

The Lady of the Lake

I t is common for things in a haunted house to be moved around. In fact, people often dismiss the first signs of a ghost because they think they misplaced something or someone else has simply moved it. They ignore the signs, even when they begin happening more frequently, because they figure their mind is playing tricks. After all, everyone has moments where they just forget where they put something.

This displacement becomes a type of gateway haunting: an intelligent haunting that involves a spirit that is still holding onto parts of its human self. This might be the first way it tries to communicate. Things might intensify because there is no response, and that's when things get scary.

The Scott House in Ocala, Florida, is well known for the ghosts that live there. As part of a larger property known as the Seven Sisters Inn, it has been the focus of ghost tours and paranormal television show crews. Most of the ghostly activity is standard for such a historic property and usually involves seeing the spirits of people who once called the land their home. For the people who come into contact with the spirits there, an old book used as a bit of décor is nothing more than a historical accent, but it proved more than that for paranormal investigator Nancy Planeta.

Nancy was more than happy to accept an invitation to investigate there in 2009, and she has since been there several more times. As a Florida resident, she has investigated dozens of haunted locations as part of the group known as The Atlantic Paranormal Society (TAPS), which is famously known as the Ghost Hunters on the hit television show of the same name. For Nancy, investigating is a mix of the evidence she can document and the occurrences she experiences. The outside world might be more interested in what

For the people who come into contact with the spirits there, an old book is nothing more than a historical accent. But it proved more than that for paranormal investigator Nancy Planeta.

The Scott House
in Ocala, Florida.

a camera can photograph or a digital audio recorder can capture, so that is what she relies on during an investigation. At the Scott House, the line between evidence and experience became blurred.

"On my first visit there, let's just say we had several strange things happen," Nancy said, "but I always look at that as 'personal experience.' " Sometimes personal experiences are more real than anything the science of investigating might be able to prove.

She was sure there were ghosts in the house. It was on that first trip that those ghosts decided to give her a gift.

"The owner had my team spend the night, which we were delighted to do. While touring the rooms, she pointed out a room called 'Sylvia's Room,' which had apparently once belonged to Mrs. Elizabeth Scott," Nancy said. The room was filled with collectibles from around the world, most of which were old and probably valuable. What really grabbed her attention was an old book sitting on the nightstand next to the bed. It was a copy of *The Lady of the Lake*, a classic poem by Sir Walter Scott chronicling

"We decided to turn on the ceiling fans. I flipped the switch and suddenly an object came flying off the fan and smacked me in the head."

the power struggles and love lives of the British royalty surrounding James V. It was perhaps the poet's most popular and critically received poem, and acted as a symbol for the realism and depth of character he wished to bring to his narrative. The edition Nancy found was not a first edition, but rather the American Book Company version that was published in 1893, making it one of the oldest American imprints of the book. It has not been confirmed, but there is speculation that Scott is actually a relative of the people who owned the property in Florida. "If not, it would be a funky coincidence," Nancy said.

She was drawn in by the age of the book and the title, which she believed was a reference to the old Arthurian legend about the spirit woman who protects the sword Excalibur and passes it on to Merlin and King Arthur.

"I picked it up and started leafing through it. (Bonnie, the owner of the house) asked why I was curious about it. I told her I wasn't sure." It struck Bonnie as well; the book was the only thing in the room that was part of the original estate of the house. It had been found in the attic and, thinking it must have been a favorite of the former owner and fitting the décor of the room, had been placed by the bed. It created the impression that Mrs. Scott was still there reading it a bit every night. Nancy put the book back on the night table and toured the rest of the house with Bonnie.

As they prepared to set up their equipment for the night, Nancy chose the loft, which was the biggest and highest room in the house, and not much more than a converted attic. "I figured that we could fit myself and the two other investigators in there with our equipment and be able to hear everything in the house below us," Nancy said.

"We settled in and turned the lights on, then realized it was warm in the room. We decided to turn on the ceiling fans. (I) flipped the switch and suddenly an object came flying off the fan and smacked me in the head." It was the book, *The Lady of the Lake*.

How had the book made it up to the loft, and more importantly, how had it gotten on one of the fan blades, another 12 feet in the air? Nancy's group and the people who worked at the house had all been part of the tour, and to her knowledge, no one had gone into the room while they walked the house or set up equipment.

"I actually shook my head at it, laughed, and said out loud, 'Funny. You're really funny, but knocking me out is not the way to get my attention.'" Not one to overlook an opportunity to communicate, Nancy and the group returned to Sylvia's room to try to get answers. They turned on their tape recorders in hopes of capturing some electronic

The Lady of the Lake, the unknown hitchhiker.

voice phenomena (EVP), in which the spirits of disembodied voices are imprinted on a recording. It seemed the perfect chance to speak with Elizabeth or whoever had left the book in the loft. They got no results.

The rest of the night was spent running up and down three flights of stairs as the paranormal activity in the house was constant. Although most of the rooms were involved in one way or another, nothing happened in Sylvia's room. They spent most of the later hours investigating happenings in the kitchen, and Sylvia's room, the loft, and the book faded from Nancy's thoughts.

"Finally, at about 5:45 a.m., we decided to try to get a few hours of sleep before we headed back. We packed up our equipment and locked the door to the loft as a precaution so housekeeping didn't wake us in the morning." The door was at the bottom of the staircase leading to the attic and was the only way in and out of the room.

The group headed home the next day. They had done the majority of packing the night before, so they were back on the road quickly and with only a few trips in and out of the loft.

"When I got home, I started unpacking," Nancy said. "As I was lifting

Whoever put the book in Nancy's bag felt she needed it. Nancy thought it was odd, but she wanted to read the book anyway and had no fear of possessing a haunted object.

my laptop out of my bag, I felt something slip and (fall on my right foot)." It was *The Lady of the Lake*. Nancy was a bit more than disturbed by this, but she took a few deep breaths and called Bonnie to tell her she had not stolen it from the room and would be bring it back.

Bonnie's response was a bit odd. She told Nancy to keep the book because it was now hers. She explained the book had found its way to the person who should have it. Whoever put it in Nancy's bag had felt she needed it somehow. Nancy thought it was odd, but she wanted to read the book anyway and had no fear of possessing a haunted object.

The book continues to play hide-and-seek with Nancy.

"Every once in a while, it will disappear from my desk in my bedroom, and reappear in the oddest places," she said. She has found the book in her refrigerator, in random places like beside the waste basket, and even inside her china cabinet. She has even brought it along during investigations, hoping that other ghosts might be drawn to it. Some believe that whatever spirit is linked to the book might be able to speak with ghosts in a different location and convince them to communicate.

Chris' epilogue: By chance, I picked up an 1895 edition of *The Lady of the Lake* for $1 at a yard sale years back. It remained unread among my mythology collection (I, too, had always thought it was a reference to the Arthurian legend), but there was something about Nancy's story that set off an alarm. I took it down after hearing her story and wondered if there was something about the book itself. Turning my digital recorder on, I flipped through the pages while asking questions and hoping for a response. Three sessions have produced nothing, but I live only a few hours away from Nancy and the Scott House, so my next test will be to take my edition to her and see if the spirits know the difference between the two books.

If *The Lady of the Lake* found its way to Nancy because she needed it somehow, maybe two copies are even better.

Her Birth Certificate

What proof is there that we exist after we die? Some say we carry on through our children and grandchildren. There also may be a legacy of the people we influenced who remember us with stories and pictures of times shared.

We live in a world of paperwork, however. There are tax returns and pay stubs and maybe diplomas hanging on a wall. There is the death certificate we never see that tells the world how we left it. But the most important document in your life is your birth certificate. Try getting a social security number or a marriage license without one. It is more than proof that you were born; it is proof that you are allowed to be counted. It makes sense, then, that some people can't let go of their birth certificates when they die.

Alice is the queen of yard sales. Give her $20 and point her in the direction of a sale, and she'll have a small fortune amassed in less than an hour.

"It's a skill. You look over little mementos of people and see something that connects," she said. "Most of the time it was just something to fill a corner in my house, but at least once a week I'd find something I could resell." While she specialized in furniture and decorations, she knew enough about antiques and appliances to make a fair amount of cash from her weekend trips.

She spotted the file cabinet one weekend a few Augusts ago. It was nothing special, just five feet of metal drawers and a lock. She was not drawn to it or even needed it, but inquired about the price because she was disappointed there weren't more items at the sale. "I felt like I needed to leave with something," she said. She stuffed the cabinet into the trunk of her car and headed home.

An empty cabinet is not much of a story, but a filled one is a story to the right person. Brimming with old bills or pictures, each drawer has something to say, and something started to speak to Alice on her way home.

The file cabinet was not an exciting buy, so Alice forgot about it, but then she started having weird dreams.

Her small car stalled at a light. She assumed it was because of the added weight of the cabinet and didn't think of it again until it stalled for a second time as she drove onto her street. "I was only a few blocks from home, so I called my husband to come and give [it] a jump. He gave me that look when he saw the cabinet hanging out of my trunk: another adventure. He calls me 'The Indiana Jones of Junk.' "

It took three tries before her husband was successful jump-starting the car. He lifted the cabinet and placed in his pickup, noticing it was heavier than expected, and waved her on. Then the truck's engine refused to start, and he blushed when he called Alice back to help him. They sat on the side of the road, less than a mile from home, giving both batteries time to charge and making fun of each other. He decided to open the file cabinet to see what was weighing it down.

"I told him there were just some hanging files and a few loose papers. He joked that it had to [hold] a weight set because he was barely able to lift it into the truck. We opened the first drawer and it had nothing in it, but the second wouldn't open."

Thinking it was locked, her husband got a screwdriver from his glove compartment to jimmy it open, but when he returned the drawer opened without any trouble. Inside were a few dozen green hanging files, none labeled. A few had colored papers in them, but most were empty. The bottom drawer opened easily but contained nothing.

When they got home, they moved the file cabinet into the mudroom until they could figure out where to place it. They still couldn't understand why it was so heavy.

"It was not a very exciting buy, so I basically forgot about it for about a week," Alice said. "Then I started to have really

The file cabinet, stored in the garage.

Alice had vivid nightmares about a woman in her kitchen. When Alice approached, the woman would turn around and try to talk. Her lips moved, but nothing came out.

weird dreams—and I don't dream."

Alice had vivid nightmares about a woman in her kitchen. She would find the stranger at her sink, as if she had just finished washing the dishes. When Alice approached, the woman would turn around and try to talk. Her lips moved but nothing came out. She would then get angry and pound on the counter, yelling without sound.

"She was beautiful," Alice said. "She was solid, not like a ghost or anything. She had long, thick black hair, but she looked like Donna Reed. Like from that era. She even had pearls and the puffy dress. All I kept thinking was she looked like a television star from a show from the '60s. She had these intense green eyes. She was very angry, though. And the worst part was she had a short temper. She'd try and be polite and then just start tearing into me."

The dreams disturbed her enough to tell her husband about them. By her own admission, she rarely remembers her dreams, so to have a recurring one certainly said something. He told her to stop watching old television shows.

When the dreams continued into a second week, he stopped laughing. Alice was beginning to lose sleep. She was scared the woman would hit her in her dream and that she would feel it in real life. She became obsessed with what the woman was trying to tell her.

"I even bought a book on lip reading. Nothing helped. The only words I could make out were, 'the kids.' I was starting to think it was someone real trying to communicate, and I started to research my house in my spare time. But nothing from that time made any bells go off."

Then the woman started to appear while Alice was awake, and that truly unnerved her. The first time occurred one evening while Alice was washing dishes. "I was doing the dishes. I emptied the garbage and left it in the mudroom to take out later. I guess I left the door open because I felt a breeze. Then I felt someone looking over my shoulder. I turned and there was the same woman. She looked at least 20 years older and was wearing a pair of old jeans and a red sweater, but it was her. Her black hair was cut into a bob, with a little gray in the corners, but not too much. She was there, staring at me. Also, I could see through her. It was not like the dream. I could see through her."

The woman looked like she had something to say, but she made no attempt to speak. She just stood there making eye contact with Alice. When the phone rang, Alice looked away for a second and the woman disappeared.

According to Alice, the whole scene lasted about half a minute. She was sure it was the same woman from her dreams.

She decided not to tell her husband. "After the way he treated the dream, there was no way I was going to tell him I was seeing this woman in the house now. I even thought I

might be going a little crazy myself," she said.

The dreams stopped, but the sightings continued. About twice a week the woman would show up, always when Alice was alone and always at night. She saw her mostly in the kitchen, but two times she woke up in the night to find the woman in the chair in the corner of the room, sitting and watching her. The woman's face was more worried and sad each time, and she always seemed to get frustrated right before she disappeared.

Alice spoke with a friend of hers who had studied ghosts. "She had a lot to say, but the thing that stuck with me was that I should try to talk to her. Right. Talk to her. I don't think so. But I took the advice," Alice said. "A few nights later, she came while I was watching TV in the living room. I was lying down on the couch with the lights on, but I wasn't asleep. I felt that cold breeze again and then a hand on my head. I knew she was there, but I couldn't see her. I said softly, 'If there is something you want from me, just let me know.' The whole room got very cold, and I could feel something sitting on my legs. I ran upstairs and jumped into bed next to my husband."

The ghost's face became distorted, like the spirit itself was being possessed by another, darker force. Alice felt hands tighten around her throat.

Alice was too scared to sleep. "I closed my eyes and refused to open them. I knew she would be there." Eventually, though, she drifted off and dreamed of walking into the kitchen to see the younger version of the ghost waiting for her. She offered her hand to Alice and led her into the mudroom. The ghost gently placed Alice's hand on the file cabinet.

"I remember [her] smile," Alice said. "At the time it was so sweet, and I felt like a kid when their mom says they did something right. I still see that smile. Now it makes me feel very scared."

When Alice woke up, she wanted to go right to the cabinet and open it up, but she was running late for work. All day she thought about it and called her friend the first chance she got. The friend said there must be something in the cabinet that was keeping the ghost trapped in this world, and offered to help Alice look through it. When she came over, she had a tape recorder. She asked the spirit to help them find what they were looking for. They searched each of the hanging files carefully, but there was nothing in them, and there was nothing in any of the other drawers.

"We didn't know what to do," Alice said.

That night in bed, Alice tossed and turned, thinking about the file cabinet and the ghost. The room filled with an "electric" feeling, and Alice tried to touch her husband's leg. It was not there.

"It felt like he had left the bed and I was there alone," she said.

Alice watched in terror as the ghost appeared in the corner of the room and ran to the bed. She remembers most how the woman's hair blew back, revealing a pair of diamond earrings. In a moment the woman was on top of her, choking her. The ghost's face became distorted, like the spirit itself was being possessed by another, darker force. Alice felt hands tighten around her throat, and her head hit the pillow repeatedly as the woman lifted her up and threw her back down. The woman finally slapped her, and disappeared as soon as her hand hit Alice's face.

"I was completely frozen. I could feel my husband next to me again. I started to shake him and he woke up and asked me what was wrong. I dragged him down into the mudroom and told him to get the cabinet out of the house. He tried to calm me down. I wanted nothing to do with it. I just wanted it out. I finally broke down and told him everything. He just nodded. I think he knew, ghost or no ghost, something was scaring me. He knew it was real to me.

"He pulled the three drawers out and found it," Alice said.

"I knew something had happened to El, that she was dead and the birth certificate meant something to her. I wondered if her husband was dead, too, and they were lost and couldn't find each other."

What they found was a New York certificate of birth for a woman Alice refuses to name. She refers to the woman only as El and says she was born in 1941. The document was issued in 1963, perhaps for a marriage license. The tattered tan paper had water stains and smeared writing. William Stern, borough registrar at the time, was listed, and there was an unidentified red mark through the rubber stamp used to make the document official.

"I knew something had happened to El, that she was dead and [the birth certificate] meant something to her. I wondered if her husband was dead, too, and somehow they were lost and couldn't find each other." She believed this was what was keeping the woman from finding peace.

Alice went back to the house where she had purchased the file cabinet.

"The man who had sold me the cabinet recognized me immediately," she said. "I think he was waiting for me to come back. As soon as he saw me, his eyes got large and he told me the cabinet had come with the house. I didn't even say anything. He just told me before I could speak. I asked if he knew anything about the family who lived there before. I'll never forget what he said. He got these real angry eyes and laughed, 'If I knew, don't you think I would have kept it?' Then he apologized and shut the door."

Alice turned to the Internet. With a name, birth date, and location, she thought she would be able to find something, but her attempts to learn anything about El stalled at every turn. She searched public records to track down the family who had lived in the house before the current resident. She found out that the previous resident had owned the house for close to 30 years. Both the mother and father had died within a year of each other, and the oldest daughter had sold the house shortly after her mother's passing. Alice tried to find the daughter but was unsuccessful, and a hunt for the cemetery where the parents were buried produced nothing.

"It was like she gave us a week," Alice said. "We tried, but it was like we were taking too long. I woke up a few more nights to find her in my room, always far away and not coming after me. Never strangled me again. She wasn't letting me sleep, I'll tell you that. Every time I would close my eyes, I knew she was there. Even if I didn't see her. Finally, I got tired of it. I yelled one night, "El, if you want me to do something, (expletive deleted) help me.'"

That night the fire alarm went off. Alice and her husband woke to find the birth certificate burning in the sink. Their first reaction was to dowse it with water, but something prevented them from doing that. They couldn't move. After it had burned away, Alice felt as if she had been punched in the stomach, but she washed the ashes down the drain.

"I never saw her again. After that, my house was my house again," Alice said.

The episode with El has gotten easier to accept over time, but there is still a fear she will come back. For Alice and her husband, it's more of a mystery than a ghost story. Why was the woman so connected to her birth certificate? Why did she ultimately destroy it, and more importantly, how was she able to?

Alice never told anyone else this story, other than her husband and her friend, but feels sharing it now will offer some closure.

"People go around looking for ghosts. I just don't get that. Maybe if they woke up to have something trying to kill them, they would think differently about it. I sometimes feel bad for that lady, not being able to find peace. Then I remember those nights I couldn't close my eyes without her messing with me. I'm glad she's gone, peace or not."

Knives and Shadow: Chris' Story

Whatever you do, don't tell this story to my wife. We have a strict policy regarding the paranormal: Keep the ghosts inside the books and outside of the house.

Loving my wife dearly, I never told her some of my experiences surrounding the occult evidence I gathered while writing my first book. To say having that evidence in my house was creepy would be an understatement. We were wary of being a depository for evidence of real murders and crimes that remained unsolved, but we struck an accord. It was "out of sight and out of mind." My wife never knew something else wanted to make sure its story got told.

In early 2004, I had an idea to write a book about Freetown, Massachusetts, a place that was the subject of rumors and whispers. I was on the trail of a good ghost story, but the more I read and researched, the more a question began to develop in my head. The resulting book, *Dark Woods: Cults, Crime, and the Paranormal in the Freetown State Forest*, became a way for me to try and answer those questions while telling a paranormal story so many locals knew, but which never seemed to make it across the town lines.

The town had a history of occult activity surrounding it. Crimes there were linked to different cults that claimed to worship Satan. Over the years, many youths were drawn to these alternative religions and practiced them in the state forest and on the Wampanoag Indian Reservation. I began to wonder if there was a connection between the paranormal activity and the cults. I contacted Alan Alves, a former detective there who at one time was one of the leading sources of information on occult crime and activity in the country.

Our first meeting ended with my car's back seat full of police files, evidence photos, and books I was told I had to read. Our second meeting a few months later resulted in a trunk full of newspaper clippings, more evidence, and the sneaking suspicion all

The young man wrote "The Lord's Prayer" backward and in his own blood.

The Bridgewater Triangle files as they were found.

was not right in southeastern Massachusetts. I carefully went through all the paperwork he had given me, trying to find some way to classify and file the different cases. It was like trying to assemble a puzzle with pieces missing and no box cover picture to guide the way.

I could tolerate photographs of graves that were robbed and small bunkers filled with ritual knives and children's clothes. But what really disturbed me was the prayer.

In the 1970s, a young man desecrated the local nativity scene. He made several cuts in his leg and poured his blood over the statues. He wrote "The Lord's Prayer" backward in the same blood. He was not connected to any group; he was just a kid who liked heavy metal music, hated authority, and struck out against the strongest group he could find. In occult circles, this activity was seen as both an offering and a prayer. The young man was eventually caught and charged with vandalism.

Alves had kept the prayer and he gave me the small piece of poster board along with the rest of the material. While Alves said nothing strange ever happened to him when he had it, after it came into my possession, it sparked.

I put the prayer in the trunk of my car under several boxes of newspaper clippings. After I arrived home and unpacked, I saw the prayer had moved on top of the boxes. I took a closer look at it. The blood had had several decades to dry and was a dirty brown, the fingerprints still clear in the strokes. It immediately made me sick, which

The bin was tipped over, files scattered, and the prayer lay a good five feet from the mess, neatly displayed on the floor. There was a kitchen knife lying across it.

was no surprise. I have no stomach for blood, and the whole idea of cult activity is too much for me.

I decided the prayer was a bit too intense to bring into the house, so I put it back in the trunk. In terms of storytelling, it was a dead end. The case had been closed and there were no reports of ghostly activity attached to it. At most, it would make a nice picture for the cult section of the book.

Two days later, while loading my car for work, I noticed the prayer was on the front seat. I assumed I had forgotten to put it back in the trunk.

That evening, I brought the prayer into the house because I was beginning to organize the materials Alves had given to me. I started to visualize what was happening in the town and wondered where the prayer fit in. For reasons I can't explain, I ended up storing the prayer under my couch. The next morning it was on top of the couch.

I called Alves and asked him if anything like this had ever happened before. He laughed at me as if to say silly little ghost hunter.

I played it safe and put the prayer in a storage bin, sealing it tight and placing other files on top of it. I woke later that night to a loud bang coming from my office. The bin was tipped over, files scattered, and the prayer lay a good five feet from the mess, neatly displayed on the floor. There was a kitchen knife lying across it.

"This is not acceptable," I whispered into the air. The last thing I wanted was my wife to wake up and see a message to Satan in my office. "You are not welcome here."

Anyone hearing me would have thought I was crazy, but I was resolved. Nothing like this had ever happened to me before. In those early days of investigating, my toolbox included a small bottle of holy water. I placed the holy water in the bin with the rest of the research materials and the prayer and went to sleep in the spare bedroom. I left the lights on.

Over the next year I submerged myself in the history of Freetown and the recent paranormal activity there. The prayer stayed in storage for the most part. I noticed it around the house from time to time, always sneaking out when my wife wouldn't find it and always accompanied by a different kitchen knife. It was clearly a message to me, but no matter how many times I tried to get someone to come clean using a tape recorder, no voice ever came through. I went from being frightened to being frustrated and annoyed. When I came home one night to find the prayer on top of a talking board I stored in a closet, complete with a knife stuck in the board, I decided I didn't want to hear whatever the prayer had to say.

Pictures I took of the prayer never seemed to turn out. I would take them in different light and from different angles, but there was always a glare. That was good enough for me—it would add to the creepiness of the picture for the book.

As with so much of the writing of that book, catastrophe hit in the final days of my work on it. My young son was playing on the computer and deleted all of the pictures I had taken for the book, including those of the prayer. I scrambled around, asking friends for anything they had, and pulled low-resolution pictures from video recordings I had made. I also tried to capture another image of the prayer for the book. Apparently the prayer did not want its picture taken again. It disappeared and did not show itself until months after the book was sent off to the publisher. This time it appeared on the floor with one of my digital cameras next to it. The batteries had been removed from the camera and placed in the shape of a cross next to the prayer.

Rehoboth, one of the most haunted towns in the Triangle.

Eventually I moved out of state and was unable to deliver the materials back to Alves before I left. The prayer stayed in a taped bin inside a storage unit for six months.

"For every step you take toward the paranormal, the paranormal takes two steps towards you," says investigator and paranormal radio personality Matt Moniz.

The prayer stayed in storage for the most part.
I noticed it around the house from time to time,
always sneaking out when my wife wouldn't
find it and always accompanied by a different
kitchen knife.

When Alves asked me to return his items, I dug deep into the unit and found them. The bin was still taped, but the prayer was neatly placed on top, despite the fact most of my possessions had been thrown around in transit. I placed all of the items in a box, making sure the prayer was on top, and shipped it back to Massachusetts.

According to Alves, when he received the box, the prayer was not in it.

The story doesn't end there, though. It continued a few years later.

Since the publication of that book, I had stored my research materials, along with all of my old files on Massachusetts, in the garage. Tim Weisberg and I broadcast a yearly radio show where local paranormal groups search the part of Massachusetts known as the Bridgewater Triangle.

One of those groups contacted me looking for a place people didn't know too much about, but would still make a splash on the show. I suggested following up on a legend at a college in the area. To locate some contact information for the group, I needed to take my research materials out of their storage cabinet in my garage. These files included evidence from the occult cases in Freetown: tapes of interviews, pictures, and books on the subject.

Although the lock on the storage cabinet has never worked, I found it locked. The cabinet itself was noticeably cold, odd considering my garage is not air-conditioned and August is a hot month in southwest Florida. I had no idea where the key was, so I went inside to get a knife to force it open. Back in the garage the light I had turned on was turned off, and the cabinet was unlocked. Better, the drawer containing the information on the Triangle was open.

A wiser man might have heeded the warning, but small moments of unusual activity are common when you study the paranormal. As investigator and paranormal radio personality Matt Moniz says, "For every step you take toward the paranormal, the paranormal takes two steps towards you."

I took the files into the kitchen, set them on the counter, and poured a cup of coffee. My daughter, two rooms away and sleeping soundly earlier, began to cry hysterically for me. I went in to soothe her and she eventually fell back asleep. When I went back to the kitchen to get my coffee and begin my search for the names, the files were scattered on the floor with a map of Freetown unfolded near them.

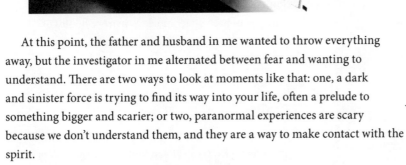

At this point, the father and husband in me wanted to throw everything away, but the investigator in me alternated between fear and wanting to understand. There are two ways to look at moments like that: one, a dark and sinister force is trying to find its way into your life, often a prelude to something bigger and scarier; or two, paranormal experiences are scary because we don't understand them, and they are a way to make contact with the spirit.

After taking several photographs to document the mess, I turned on a tape recorder and began to talk to whomever might be there, hoping someone was trying to break through. The session produced no results, so I carried the files into my office and went to bed. As I tried to fall asleep, I heard bangs coming from my office.

The next morning the files were where I left them, so I considered the whole thing over. That night, however, as I tried to send e-mails to my contacts, my computer shut down. When I work on ghost stories, my computer sometimes goes haywire—an example of how electrical items can malfunction because of paranormal activity. Then the lights in the living room went off. I switched computers, sent the e-mails, and placed the files back in my office. The lights flickered a few more times, but the activity stopped for the most part.

The contacts got back to me and I relayed the information to the group. However, a hurricane hit New England, preventing them from researching the legend at the college.

My paperwork, now permanently stored in the unlocked file cabinet in my garage, can hardly be blamed for the weather 1,700 miles away. Right?

The Psychic, the Little Girl, and Three Killers

Where does a psychic go when she is looking for a little peace of mind? Jackie Barrett, who has worked on cases involving Amityville murderer Ronald DeFeo, Jr., and counsels people like convicted killer Damon Eckles of the West Memphis 3, goes to one of the most haunted bed and breakfasts in the country.

Lizzie Borden.

This story goes back generations. When the bodies of Andrew Borden and his second wife, Abby, were found on Aug. 6, 1892, all eyes in the community turned to Andrew's daughter, Lizzie. What happened over the next year became the subject of legend. Lizzie Borden was arrested and tried for hacking up her father, a wealthy pillar of the community, and her stepmother. The murders were so brutal they shocked a nation still reeling from the violence of such serial killers as Jack the Ripper and Dr. H. H. Holmes. The Borden family's dirty laundry was aired, but Lizzie inherited the family money and was able to afford the best attorneys. On June 20, 1893, she was found not guilty and released from jail.

For the next 100 years, as new details of the case came out and others got painted over, Lizzie Borden reached the status of folk hero. Kids skipped rope to the famous song, "*Lizzie Borden took an ax...*" Movies were made and plays were written about her. The details of what exactly happened that day in 1892 became distorted as everyone attempted to solve the mystery.

Meanwhile, the house in which the murders took place was gaining a reputation of its own. Located at 92 Second Street in Fall River, Massachusetts, the house passed through different owners. At one time a business was attached to it, and at another time the property was expanded. All the while, people were experiencing various types of paranormal activity there.

Tragedy was nothing new to this house, which had witnessed murders even *before* the Bordens lived there. The people being haunted never knew whether it was the murdered family or one of the other victims knocking on walls, moving things, or crying in the night.

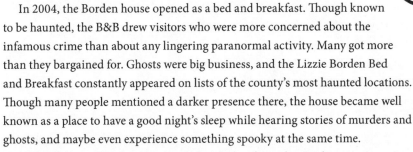

The original Borden house, below, and as it is today, at left, as the Lizzie Borden Bed and Breakfast.

In 2004, the Borden house opened as a bed and breakfast. Though known to be haunted, the B&B drew visitors who were more concerned about the infamous crime than about any lingering paranormal activity. Many got more than they bargained for. Ghosts were big business, and the Lizzie Borden Bed and Breakfast constantly appeared on lists of the county's most haunted locations. Though many people mentioned a darker presence there, the house became well known as a place to have a good night's sleep while hearing stories of murders and ghosts, and maybe even experience something spooky at the same time.

Jackie Barrett, who grew up exposed to dark cults and specializes in recreating violent crimes to help gather evidence, took a roundabout path to Fall River. After working for years as a psychic and life advisor, she'd seen just about everything. As someone who can tap into energy to see crimes that have happened in a specific location, she was often called upon to look for victims and suspects of murder cases. One of these cases involved a young girl, who was viciously murdered in

People believe ghosts often stay until any unfinished business is settled, but even after the real murderer was caught, the little girl remained with Jackie.

After getting the documents, Jackie's cat mysteriously died. Over the course of working with DeFeo, three other pets died.

a suburb of Philadelphia. Although the police arrested a suspect and put him in jail, many involved in the case felt the wrong man ended up behind bars. People related to the case, including police investigators and court workers, saw the dead girl walking through their houses. She was always wearing a nightgown like the one she was buried in, although now it was dirty. "She was usually crying. These hard-nosed people, cops and lawyers, couldn't get the case out of their heads," Jackie said.

Through her work, they were able to find the real killer, which opened up a can of worms with other unsolved murders in the area. While the work of a psychic is often exhausting, this case was especially hard for Jackie, who was in almost constant contact with the dead girl.

"I was with her every night," she said. "Sometimes she wanted to talk and sometimes she wanted to play. It was constant. But I felt connected to her, and I wanted to help."

People believe ghosts often stay until any unfinished business is settled, but even after the real murderer was caught, the little girl remained with Jackie. "And I let her. I could handle it better than the other people she was going to," she said.

While at a conference near the end of the case, she ran into Lee-Ann Wilber, manager of the Lizzie Borden Bed and Breakfast. Wilber suggested Jackie come to the Borden house to try to communicate with the ghosts there.

"I needed a change of scenery, a vacation, so I decided to go," Jackie said.

In November 2005, Jackie made the trip to Massachusetts. Before leaving, she invited the ghost girl to go along with her. Even during the journey there, she sensed the presence of the little girl.

During Jackie's two days at the house, she and her companions had their own paranormal experiences: Her husband has held down in bed during an afternoon nap, they caught glimpses of a ghost cat, and during a séance, the spirit of Bridget Sullivan, the Borden's maid at the time of the murders, spoke through a woman who had come to visit.

Jackie and her husband were completely convinced there were ghosts in the house, and when they departed, they left another spirit behind: The little ghost girl.

Jackie has never been able to completely understand the little girl's reason for staying, or even if her soul had just moved on, but she never saw her again. No one else related to the murder investigation has seen her either. There is some evidence, however, that she may be trapped at the famous bed and breakfast.

The people who run the bed and breakfast stock their bookcase shelves with every book on the subject of Lizzie. People who stay there can read every theory of the crime or hear any of a number of ghost stories about the place. Before she left, Jackie added her own contribution to the collection, a copy of her book, *The House That Kay Built*. It is not about Lizzie in any way, but it added to the overall spookiness of the house. The trouble was that the book did not stay in the bookcase.

It began to pop up in various locations throughout the house. Although visitors rarely removed it from its shelf, the book mysteriously appeared on chairs, beds, and even on the kitchen table. Though always returned to the bookcase, it disappeared and reappeared frequently.

A newcomer to the house solved the mystery. Ben was a high school senior when he began working at the bed and breakfast. When *The House That Kay Built* appeared on top of a toy chest, he made a connection. He believed a number of child spirits trapped in the house wanted to be read to, and because there were so few children's books in the house, he read to them from Jackie's work. He noticed that the book moved around more frequently when he was working, and when he read the book, activity in other parts of the house decreased. It was as if the spirits of the children were listening to him read instead of roaming the halls. Ben became a common site, reading aloud to the young spirits until he enrolled in college and quit working at Lizzie's.

Jackie is not sure what to make of it all. Some of the first reports of hauntings at the bed and breakfast involved the original children who died on the property, drowned by their own insane mother, a distant relative of Lizzie's.

There is nothing about the haunted book that specifically points to her little girl spirit, but Jackie doesn't live her life by facts alone. "Part of the reason I invited her to come was so she could play with the other kids trapped in the house. She never got to play with other kids when she was alive. I like to think she is just telling me she stayed and is happy there," Jackie said.

Jackie gets another message, too—the girl wants her to come back—but a part of her doesn't trust the messenger. During her many paranormal experiences, she has been lured to locations and situations by dark forces, and what walks that property is not always truthful.

"I think they have her trapped," Jackie said. She believes something stronger (although she refuses to say *demonic*) may have started all the trouble on the property and that it remains there. She also thinks they either kidnapped the girl ghost to use her energy and light, or to get Jackie to come back. "It's a fun place to go, but there is also something not fun about it," she said.

Darker forces have found other ways to get into Jackie's life. Through a series of bizarre events, Jackie came to possess boxes of evidence, court documents, and personal correspondence of Ronnie "Butch" DeFeo, the man who murdered his family in the famous "Amityville Horror" house. His killings made the price of the house fall so low it became attractive to the Lutz family, who moved in and eventually had to move out because of the evil spirits there.

While the Lutz family and their experiences have been open to scrutiny, no one can dispute that DeFeo's family was murdered in the house. Over the years, there have been whispers that Ronnie was possessed at the time of the murders, that he made a pact with the devil, and that there was something about the man and the house that was evil.

Jackie was drawn to Ronnie before she knew who he was, almost as if he was whispering in her ear. She eventually began to correspond with him and then met him face-to-face. Trust and bonds were formed, or to hear Jackie tell it, reformed.

"Ronnie gave me power of attorney to help him. He was very ill, and I agreed to get him medical attention. And Ronnie gave me his story," she said.

Along with the story came the paperwork of a lifetime as well as court documents, stored in a room in the Amityville house, which told the other side of one of the most famous cases in paranormal history. But when Jackie got the papers, something else came along with them.

Bad things began to happen. Jackie, who was used to seeing spirits, saw darker things than she was accustomed to seeing. In the matter of a few weeks after getting the documents, her cat mysteriously died. Over the course of working with DeFeo, three other pets died and he seemed to have knowledge about some of them.

People around her were getting seriously

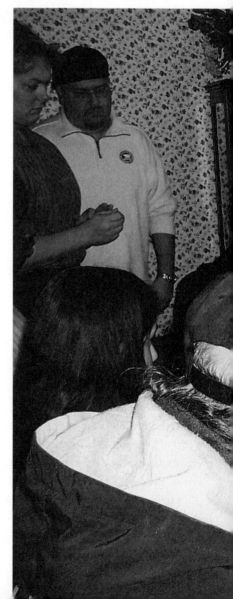

sick without explanation, and she herself was suffering from a physical and emotional attack. "I had things come into my own mind and questioned my own sanity," she said.

Through working with the murderer, she unlocked doors to her past that had been shut tight for decades. She and Ronnie were destined to be together.

"I saw this face come through a wall when I was a child," Jackie said. "I realized now (his) was the face I saw. Ronnie knew things about me no one else knew."

She began to receive phone calls from him at all hours of the night,

Jackie (wearing a scarf) at the séance at the Lizzie Borden Bed and Breakfast.

> "I keep seeing these dark people in my house.
> I see them in mirrors and the windows. I see
> them just walking around and hiding."

something nearly impossible because inmates at a prison, especially ones serving multiple murder convictions, do not have access to phones. The caller ID would never display the prison's name, and most of the area codes were not from New York, where he is incarcerated. Jackie believes Ronnie was able to travel in different ways outside of his body. One way was through phone lines; another was through dark spirits who were with him the night of the murders and continued to be with him until recently.

"He had entities all around him," she said.

Jackie now believes part of the connection she had with Ronnie was due to his documents stored at her house. However, she is much more disturbed by the new spirits roaming her house.

"There is always something happening here. I keep seeing these dark people in my house. I see them in mirrors and the windows. I see them just walking around and hiding. People don't come to me like that. I can't talk to them. They are coming all the time, and I can't talk to them," she said.

The Amityville House as it looks today.

Chris' epilogue: Whether the files are cursed or haunted, or whether there is just something odd about the case, DeFeo's entities didn't stop with Jackie. She called me, looking for advice. As we were talking, the phone line went dead twice. At one point during the conversation, I went online to look up some of the things she was talking about, and my computer shut down.

She asked me if I would be willing to help her write the book about Ronnie. Having written about criminals before, and having received multiple letters from people in prison, I was hesitant to say yes. In addition to exposing my family to the criminal aspects of the case, I was unsure if I wanted to work on a book about someone who had been written about so often and who faced possible legal action because of what he was going to say. I also felt as if I was stepping onto a paranormal mine field. I was already experiencing odd things, and all we were doing was talking. I told her I probably would not get involved.

But Ronnie had other ideas. That night, I saw several black figures roaming around, and one walked into my room as I was falling asleep. I moved out to the couch so I wouldn't wake my wife. Then my computer turned back on. At one point a loud noise shook the house, as if something large had dropped in my office.

Jackie believes she has freed Ronnie of the demons that plagued him.

Over the next week, I began receiving phone calls at all hours of the day, most with no number listed on the caller ID. A few displayed "New York State." I always picked up, but no one was ever on the line.

At the end of October 2010, Jackie talked about the case on our radio show, "Spooky Southcoast." Everything on my end began to malfunction. My computer would shut down or I would lose work I had done about her. The show aired without a hitch, but I suffered through several power outages throughout my whole house while it was broadcast.

The next night—Halloween—a documentary about her work and her struggle to free Ronnie from demons aired on cable TV. I set my DVR to record it, but the electricity went out again. I recorded a later broadcast, but when I attempted to watch it, my television kept shutting off. Eventually it was deleted and I never saw it.

My mind was made up: I would leave this case alone.

Jackie did not. She pressed on and believes she has freed Ronnie of the demons that plagued him, and has written a book about it: *The Devil I Know: My Haunting Journey with Ronnie DeFeo and the True Story of the Amityville Murders*. Since his deliverance, the hauntings have stopped.

Jackie continues to study the paranormal. That is her life, and however dark or intimidating it gets, she is a survivor and always makes it through.

Those boxes of documents are still in her house, and her first book continues to grace the bookcase in the Lizzie Borden Bed and Breakfast. They are part of a bigger picture we can't see with normal eyes. Even Jackie, who sees more than we ever will, can't take it all in.

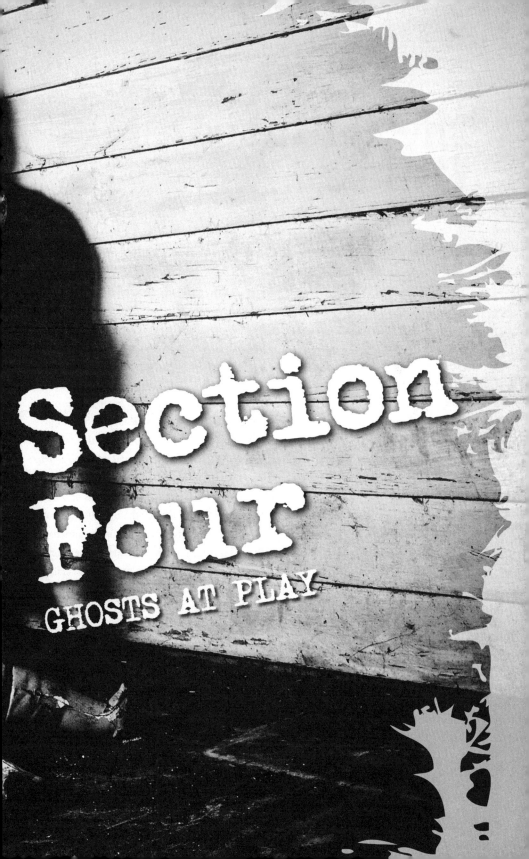

Section Four

GHOSTS AT PLAY

The Haunted Violin

There is nothing more haunting than the sound of violin music, especially when the violin itself is haunted.

Harold Gordon Cudworth, a violinist extraordinaire and collector of such instruments, was a popular musician in Massachusetts in the 1930s and 1940s, even hosting his own radio program and making at least one known recording. Yet despite his impressive body of work, Cudworth was perhaps even more famous for the instrument he played, rather than the grace with which he played it.

The story of his haunted violin was well known throughout the small town of Wareham, situated between Plymouth and Cape Cod, even before it appeared in a few volumes of New England legends and lore, including Curt Norris' *Ghosts I Have Known*, Robert Ellis Cahill's *New England's Ghostly Haunts*, a compilation of ghost stories from *Yankee Magazine* titled "Mysterious New England," and *The Haunted Violin: True New England Ghost Stories*, a collection of ghostly tales by Wareham native Edward Lodi.

Cudworth was a discerning player and favored the finely crafted instruments of the Italian masters. He eschewed the more modern violins of his day for the ornate, antiquated versions that had once been carved for royalty and nobility. In fact, Cudworth claimed he knew the "secrets" of such legendary crafters as Antonio Stradivari and Guarneri del Gesu, and how they created such lush sounds from their instruments, even if such claims were more showmanship than supernatural. (Scientific experimentation has revealed in recent years, albeit somewhat controversially, that the chemicals used to treat the wood are responsible for the tones.) Cudworth had amassed quite an impressive collection, yet his favorite was a German model from 1769 crafted by Joseph Hornsteiner.

It was the Hornsteiner violin that he was playing one day in the kitchen of his mother's home in Wareham. As he played the tune, "The Broken Melody," a rumbling sound came from the sink. It seemed to stop and start in conjunction with his playing. The phenomenon was repeated in other residences and locations as well. Sometimes when Cudworth played the song, nothing supernatural happened; other times, pictures would rock on the wall and objects would fly across the room.

This took place off and on for over 20 years, including in Cudworth's own home. In one particular instance, the banging of the latch on the attic door was so severe that Cudworth

Sometimes when Cudworth played the song, nothing supernatural happened; other times, pictures would rock on the wall and objects would fly across the room.

He had played no more than a single note before the sky grew dark and foreboding and the violin began to play a haunting tune all on its own.

went upstairs to investigate. When he did, he noticed the door of his music cabinet was open and the sheet music to "The Broken Melody" was left for him to find.

When a group of newspaper reporters led by Norris invited Cudworth to play the tune at the newspaper offices, it set off unexplainable noises throughout the vacant parts of the building and left the reporters scratching their heads. Cudworth, who according to Lodi didn't believe in ghosts himself, was convinced that something was accompanying his playing. He passed away in 1989, and the Hornsteiner was presumably auctioned with the rest of Cudworth's collection. Its whereabouts are currently unknown.

Some might argue that the spirits were not attached to the violin, but rather to Cudworth himself. Why, then, would they only manifest during the playing of one particular tune?

It could have been the tune itself. "The Broken Melody" was composed by English cellist Auguste Van Biene in 1892, and became a smash hit that he himself played more than 6,000 times until he died mid-performance in January 1913. Was the spirit associated with Cudworth's performances that of Van Biene, acknowledging the lasting legacy of his composition?

Even if Cudworth's Hornsteiner was indeed haunted, it's certainly not the first instance of the supernatural being associated with the violin.

'Devil's Trill Sonata'

There is a story from Germany in the 12th century that is recounted in Howard Schwartz's *Lilith's Cave: Jewish Tales of the Supernatural* (Oxford University Press, 1988), in which a carpenter is asked to make a coffin and uses the one remaining board to carve a fine violin. As he worked on the violin and its bow over a few days, he was visited in his dreams each night by the dead man for whom he had constructed the coffin. Each time, the man warned him against creating the violin.

The carpenter, enamored with his handiwork, did not heed the dead man's warnings. He finished the instrument and immediately drew up the bow to the strings. He had played no more than a single note before the sky grew dark and foreboding and the violin began to play a haunting tune all on its own. The man ran to the window to see what had brought upon such darkness, and as soon as he did, two invisible hands pushed him out the window and into some quicksand below, where he sunk to his suffocating death.

Yet the next morning, the carpenter's son found his father's dead body not in a sand pit, but right on the floor of his workshop, the violin next to him.

Another ghastly legend suggests that if you place a violin in a quiet room on Halloween and drop a lone piece of candy or some other offering into the F-hole, the faint sounds of the "Devil's Trill Sonata" can be heard in the air.

That particular composition also has a legend of its own. Actually titled "Violin Sonata in G Minor," it was composed by Giuseppe Tartini in 1713, after the devil came to him in a dream.

Tartini recounted the story to French astronomer Jerome Lalande, who printed the composer's own words in Lalande's 1765 work, *Voyage d'un Francois en Italie*:

"One night, in the year 1713, I dreamed I had made a pact with the devil for my soul. Everything went as I wished: My new servant anticipated my

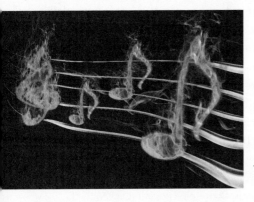

every desire. Among other things, I gave him my violin to see if he could play. How great was my astonishment on hearing a sonata so wonderful and so beautiful, played with such great art and intelligence, as I had never even conceived in my boldest flights of fantasy. I felt enraptured, transported, enchanted: My breath failed me, and I awoke. I immediately grasped my violin in order to retain, in part at least, the impression of my dream. In vain! The music which I at this time composed is indeed the best that I ever wrote, and I still call it the 'Devil's Trill,' but the difference between it and that which so moved me is so great that I would have destroyed my instrument and have said farewell to music forever if it had been possible for me to live without the enjoyment it affords me."

Although the "Devil's Trill Sonata" is considered to be one of the most beautiful and technically advanced pieces ever composed for the violin, Tartini himself said that it paled in comparison to what the Devil had played in his dream:

"(It) was so inferior to what I heard that if I could have subsisted on other means, I would have broken my violin and abandoned music forever."

Shades of Tartini's dream is echoed in even more contemporary pieces, such as The Charlie Daniels Band's 1979 hit, "The Devil Went Down to Georgia," in which Old Scratch is a "fiddler" of great skill.

Even today, a direct connection exists between the supernatural and the violin. There exists a psychoacoustic phenomenon in which a musician plays two simultaneous tones and a third tone, whose frequency is the sum or difference of the two tones being played, can be heard as well. Tartini was the first to discover this anomaly, and so they are known as Tartinin tones.

Or, more commonly, they're called "ghost tones."

Robert's Rules:
Chris' Experience with the
World's Most Haunted Doll

Throughout the history of the ghost story and the horror movie, the haunted doll is the symbol of creepiness, and a classic image of a haunted item.

The mere mention of one makes people shiver, causing them to remember movie scenes like the ones from *Poltergeist* or *Magic*, or *The Twilight Zone*'s Talky Tina. It also reminds them of a dark night from their own childhood, when a trusted toy didn't quite look right in the shadows.

It's easy to see why. The dead eyes and frozen expressions make them alive enough to talk if we spend enough time with them. They sit in the corner of the room, watching us, and then do whatever they please when we aren't around. After all, how often do we remember where or how they were positioned before we left the room or fell asleep?

If dolls are the cornerstone of haunted items, then Robert would have to be the cornerstone of haunted dolls. That's no surprise to him. He's been haunting people and inspiring nightmares since he was first made in 1904, and if you believe the stories of his birth, he is doing just what he was made to do.

The story goes that there was tension between Robert Eugene Otto, a famous artist in Key West, Florida, and one of his servants. She was fired, and in her anger she turned to the voodoo she learned as a young child and continued to practice in secret. To prove there were no hard feelings, she built a doll for Otto's young son, Robert Jr., in his image. However, she cursed it upon leaving. Shortly after being given the doll, also named Robert, the young son asked to be called Eugene, to distinguish himself from the doll.

Not long after entering Eugene's life, Robert the doll took on a life on its own. Eugene became obsessed with the doll, playing with it and carrying it everywhere. A second voice was often heard when the two were playing together. Items around the house would disappear or be found smashed, or toys of Eugene's would be destroyed, and little Eugene would be blamed for the mishap. He would object, telling his parents, "Robert did it." The catchphrase stuck.

Not long after entering Eugene's life,
Robert the doll took on a life on its own.

A display of Robert paraphernalia.

People claimed to see the doll move—sometimes just its head, other times its whole body. It would appear in different windows of the house and smile out at the neighbors. In one story, family members say they saw it running through the house.

Graves and Gravestones, a local ghost tour that has permission to visit Robert at night, says the activity did not stop there. When Robert Otto died, Eugene inherited the house. Into adulthood, he remained close to the doll. Walking around with it and seating it at the dinner table led to the disintegration of his marriage. Eugene's wife kept putting Robert out of sight, but the doll kept coming back, often visiting her.

When Eugene died in 1974, Robert was hidden in the attic and eventually discovered by the people who bought the house, the contract of which specified keeping the doll on the property.

Robert's new home, the East Martello Museum.

The family's daughter loved the doll at first, but its activities proved too much for her. She cried when the doll moved around her room, and told her parents it wanted her dead. On several occasions, she said it even attempted to choke her. The creepiness of those incidents, including a time when the doll was found sitting at the foot of the bed holding a knife, forced the people to finally get rid of it. The doll was moved to the East Martello Museum on the edge of Key West, where it remains today.

Robert doesn't seem to be getting any nicer in retirement, although it gets harder to separate legend from any real effect the doll has on the people around it.

Robert sometimes is removed from the museum and brought on tour around the Keys. When Robert was taken to a conference in Clearwater, Florida, a few years ago, story has it the doll demanded to ride in the front seat, wear a seat belt, and have a bed of its own in the hotel.

I attended the same conference, sitting at a table selling books, and was maybe 10 feet away from the doll. Most of my day was spent taking pictures of people who wanted to be seen with Robert. Near the end of the day, when I had to tell visitors (mostly children) that Robert was done for the day, their faces fell. People ran from all corners of the hotel to say goodbye to the doll when it was removed from its glass display and put in a case for transportation back to the museum. They all chanted Robert's name wildly.

If you think this is just a story to get you to visit the East Martello Museum and pay the price of admission, people will tell you otherwise. Their stories have become part of the mysticism surrounding the toy.

"Robert's Rules" are simple to follow, but most people want to be part of the ghost story, and disrespecting the doll is the quickest way to become part of the legend.

Visitors to the museum are asked to obey three rules, known as "Robert's Rules": You must say hello to the doll when you enter; ask its permission before you take a picture of it; and say thank you and good-bye when you leave. They are simple rules to follow; however, most people want to be part of the ghost story, and disrespecting the doll is the quickest way to become part of the legend. They snap pictures without first asking permission, and hope to see odd things in the view screens of their digital cameras.

The real testament to Robert's supernatural abilities, or the ability for rational people to replace coincidence with superstition, concerns the alcove wall behind the doll. Visitors from across the country and beyond write to Robert, and the best letters get displayed on the wall. People write to thank Robert for their experiences and to tell the doll what they have been up to. This is not typical fan mail, however. Most of the letters are apologies to

The Ghost and Gravestone's tour bus in Key West, Florida.

Most of the letters are apologies to Robert for not following the doll's rules. The letter writers claim bad things have happened to them and all basically say the same thing: I didn't believe, bad things happened, please forgive me.

Robert for not following the rules. The letter writers claim bad things have happened to them since their visit, usually occurring right after seeing Robert. Written in everything from shaky penmanship to thoughtful calligraphy to typed precision, the letters all basically say the same thing: *I didn't believe, bad things happened, please forgive me.*

The beauty of Robert is that he acts as a rational touchstone for irrational ideas. Through Robert, people indulge the part of themselves that is entertained by "looking under the bed." After all, the fear of dolls is as innocent as youth. As an adult, you can visit Robert and pretend for a few minutes that you've gotten over that childhood fear. You can embrace and conquer it at the same time.

Most interesting is the culture that has developed around Robert. The doll is promoted on nearly everything: its blank expression is seen in framed pictures and adorns buttons, coffee cups, license plates, drink cozies, shirts … all accompanied by the catchphrase, "Robert did it!"

Robert is also big business for local tour companies. While all of the tours around Key West point out where the doll was created and where it is currently located, only one, Graves and Gravestones, actually has permission to go into the museum after hours and schedule more intimate showings. According to David Casey, manager of the tour company, Robert's draw has made it the most popular tour in town. Since starting in 2010, the company runs two tours daily (four daily during the tourist season), and most people come to see Robert. "He's a major draw. Everybody asks about him and we've built the tour around him," Casey said.

Of course, the whole situation is set up to give people the haunted moment they crave, and that's part of the fun. The guides, for example, give the tourists EMF meters when they enter the museum, but do not explain the proper way to use them or what the electromagnetic field really is. The tourists get excited as they swing the meters around and gasp when they go off.

Even Robert's Rules invite horrible evidence for investigators, while providing memories for visitors. Robert is surrounded by thick, clear plastic that reflects light in all directions, a trick that may well be intentional. It nearly always produces something in a photograph you don't think should be there. Tourists snap their pictures quickly without asking Robert for permission, getting all sorts of illusions.

Robert draws visitors to the museum from all parts of the country. This means the

The author snapped this photo of Robert before asking
permission and far enough to catch the lights and flash.

The beauty of Robert is that he acts as a rational touchstone for irrational ideas. Through Robert, people indulge the part of themselves that is entertained by "looking under the bed."

This is the photo the author got of Robert after the doll granted permission.

Good luck from Robert.

souls who visit the doll and break its rules are more likely to have travel mishaps than others. One woman, who traveled by plane, lost her luggage. Another suffered a car accident on her way home. Still another had her computer stolen. All of these incidents would have been dismissed had they not occurred after seeing Robert first. Breaking the doll's rules explains away the everyday bad luck we have.

Robert's life continues in the digital world. There's a Robert blog you can follow, and a daily count of all of the batteries the doll has drained. There is an endless trail of websites devoted to Robert, and innumerable ghost stories that recount the doll's tale.

The official website, www.robertthedoll.org, claims teachers are using the doll in the classroom, something I have done on occasion in my middle school writing and reading classes. There are more YouTube videos of the doll than most celebrities, and the web hits, videos, and stories continue to grow.

As I write this, it is the beginning of the Christmas season, and my mother has promised a doll for my young daughter. It is from a company that specializes in making dolls that look like the little girl they are being given to, so in the next few weeks, there

I got over my fear of dolls years ago, even though my sister tortured me with wild tales of Barbie dolls waking at night and trying to kill me.

Letters to the doll, both good and bad.

will be two versions of my daughter hanging around.

At some point, I know the doll and I will be alone in the house. My daughter might leave the doll in the living room where, feeling safe from the spirits I write about, I usually pen my ghost stories. I might look over and see it smiling at me, but I'm not afraid. I got over my fear of dolls years ago, even though my sister tortured me with wild tales of Barbie dolls waking at night and trying to kill me.

Yet, I have seen many strange things since I began studying paranormal activity and I know there are any number of situations that could cause an object to move, or a plastic head to turn. I know I will never stop by my daughter's room, with door closed and lights off, and hear a strange voice answering her questions.

This could never happen. This could never happen.

Claire the Doll

When Jill was eight years old, she was given an old porcelain doll by a dear family friend, Miss Marian. The kindly old woman was always dropping by Jill's home and leaving her gifts, and this doll was the last thing she gave her before she passed away.

Jill was never really into dolls, but was delighted to have a new keepsake from her beloved friend. She gave the doll a place of honor, seating it in a child-sized rocking chair beside the nightlight.

The doll was rather pretty, with pink lips, brown eyes, and rosy peach cheeks. Dark brown hair hung in slightly frizzled and now-loose curls. It wore a peach and cream-colored dress with apron and petticoats and little black Mary Jane shoes that, when removed, showed delicately painted toenails. The doll's body was soft fabric, and its head, forearms, hands, and legs from the knees down were porcelain.

The doll looked almost like Jill. In fact, Miss Marian made a point of saying the doll reminded her of young Jill, and that's why she gave it to her. While there was definitely a strong resemblance between the girl and the plaything, perhaps Miss Marian had other reasons for wanting the doll out of her own home.

Jill named the doll Claire, and from the moment it entered her house, frightening things began to happen.

"I was always uneasy with Claire," Jill said. "I never wanted to touch her, and when I played in my room, it was as if she was watching me. It wasn't anything to panic about, but I do remember feeling like if I did something wrong, she might actually tell on me. How ridiculous does that sound?"

The activity surrounding Claire began one night when Jill was reading in her room—a book of ghost stories, perhaps not coincidentally. She was jarred by the sound of the carousel horse that sat on her dresser springing to musical life. It wasn't just a few odd notes, like an old mechanical music box is known to emit from a slight vibration to its pedestal, but the entire song, as if it was fully wound.

Jill named the doll Claire, and from the moment it entered her house, frightening things began to happen.

Claire the doll, with unblinking stare.

Perhaps the strangest incident following the doll's arrival was the day Miss Marian found a set of gold teeth in her toilet.

Jill sat there in disbelief, watching the little horse move up and down in time with the music. This couldn't be happening; even her eight-year-old mind knew that. She wasn't afraid as much as she was shocked. Then, as quickly as it had started, the music and the horse just stopped.

"I was a pretty brave kid. I didn't run and tell my mom," said Jill. She'd seen a figure she called the Shadow Man throughout her life, but her parents never believed her, so she simply stopped talking about it. "If [Mom] wouldn't believe me about that, she wouldn't believe anything as mundane as a music box, so I just let it go."

Not long after that incident came the voice. For several nights, Jill was awakened by a woman several inches from her face, shouting, "Jill! Wake up!" Jill instantly jumped out of bed, only to find her room empty.

Although the woman shouting her name died down after a few months, the phenomena moved on to her younger brother. After they were both grown and out of the house, the woman started screaming in her father's face while he slept, and she still does to this day.

But even with the woman no longer shouting her awake at night, other little things began to happen. Jill would put an item in a certain place, only to find it later on the floor right in front of the doll. Any item that went missing—and many did—would end up near Claire. One time, Jill even found a missing ring in the pocket of the doll's apron. Other strange things occurred around the doll as well—books fell off shelves and a perfume scent enveloped the room without any verifiable cause.

The night that changed Jill's opinion of Claire from benign trickster to malevolent force sounds like something straight out of a horror movie. She awoke to thumping sounds coming from near her closet. Her sleepy eyes were drawn to the nightlight in the corner of the room, and to the rocking chair in which Claire sat. Terror gripped her as she saw where the thumping sound was coming from—the rocking chair was swaying back and forth on its own.

Staring at the doll, Jill saw its feet, which had previously been pointed in opposite directions, slowly straighten themselves until they were both pointing up. In a moment of horror that still haunts Jill's nightmares to this day, the doll turned its

head toward Jill (which should have been an impossibility, since it was affixed to her cloth body), its lifeless eyes staring straight into her soul.

At that exact moment, all four music boxes in Jill's room began to play in a full-out cacophony of creepiness. Jill was frozen with fear and screamed out for her parents. As soon as she did, the music boxes all stopped at once, although Claire continued to stare at Jill.

The place where Claire was kept.

Yet even after that, Jill couldn't bring herself to get rid of Claire. She stuffed the doll in a box in the back of a storage closet and never allowed another one in her room.

Even though Jill thought about Claire over the years, it wasn't until she shared this story with me that she realized a connection between Claire and Miss Marian that might explain the spirit attached to the doll.

Miss Marian had sworn that the house she lived in was haunted by the spirits of the victims of a horrendous train accident that happened less than a mile from her home in 1900. Thirty-eight people died, as the train plunged into a flooded creek.

Miss Marian was never quite sure where the doll came from. She found it while cleaning out a closet and had no recollection of ever buying it or receiving it as a gift.

Miss Marian placed the doll on a shelf, and soon weird things began happening—cigar smoke materializing and blowing in her face, disembodied voices and footsteps coming from the basement, and glass breaking with no shards to be found. Perhaps the strangest incident following the doll's arrival was the day Miss Marian found a set of gold teeth in her toilet. Miss Marian also reported nights in which she would be tucked into bed by unseen hands. The doll was known to move on

Dolls are meant to be loved by the little girls who care for them. Claire, however, was probably meant to be right where Jill put it - in a box in the back of a storage closet. Forever.

its own throughout the house, from shelf to stool to sofa, all with no explanation as to how it got there.

The doll could have been possessed by the spirit of one of the victims of the train wreck, or maybe it was even on the train when the accident happened. Perhaps it was the cause of the accident. If a doll can tuck an elderly woman into bed and make music boxes perform on command, who is to say it couldn't also force a train to plunge into the murky depths of a swelled creek?

Dolls are meant to be a thing of beauty, to be treasured and played with and loved by the little girls who care for them. Claire, however, was probably meant to be right where Jill put it—in a box in the back of a storage closet. Forever.

Tim's epilogue: After sharing this story with me and after a great deal of convincing, Jill agreed to send Claire to me for experimentation. On the day the doll arrived, packed neatly in a cardboard box and delivered by UPS, I asked the driver if anything strange had happened while the package was in transit. He said nothing out of the ordinary occurred.

I took the box to my kitchen table and removed Claire. I had an EMF detector on the table as well, ready to measure any potential disturbances in the electromagnetic field. The needle on the meter spiked as soon as I lifted the doll out of the box and placed it on the table, but quickly returned to its base reading. Frequent testing with the EMF meter for the next few weeks produced no further spikes.

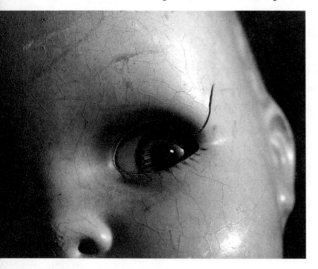

That first night, I brought Claire with me to record the sports show I produce. I took the doll into our studio, placing it on the edge of a long conference table out of the camera's view. Yet during the show, we experienced strange double-exposures of our video while it was recording, something that had never occurred before. It only happened on one of the three cameras we used, and I couldn't duplicate it again after the show was finished.

I attempted numerous EVP sessions to see if I could record any ghostly voices coming from Claire, with no results. I did, however, once hear a conversation coming from my home office where I kept the doll. It sounded like two distinct voices, male and female. When I got to the office, they stopped talking.

While working on this book late one night, I heard a scratching sound coming from the corner of the room...

A few other strange occurrences took place as well. There is a wall separating my home office from the living room. While working on this book late one night, I heard a scratching sound coming from the corner of the room, along the wall that connects to the living room. I searched all around but found nothing. A few nights later, my wife was home alone and told me she, too, heard a scratching sound but could not discover the source. As far as we know, there are no pests in our walls, attic, or basement, and the scratching noises stopped when I moved Claire to another part of the office.

Also, there were a few instances in which the heat in my office mysteriously turned on. The office is on a different heating zone than the rest of the house—the room was an addition to the original structure—and it has its own thermostat. I never turn the thermostat up in the office because heat from the main zone is usually enough to warm the room.

During the last few weeks of writing this book, we were enjoying a warmer-than-usual late autumn in the Northeast, and the 60-degree days and 40-degree nights required no additional help from my oil burner. Yet one day we arrived home to be blasted by warm air; the thermostat in the office, which is behind a computer desk and hard to reach, was turned to its highest setting. I turned it off. A few days later, it seemed warm in there again, and when I looked at the thermostat, it had been turned to about 70 degrees. Nobody in our family had touched it. I began to wonder if perhaps Claire, who spent all those years tucked away in a closet, was feeling a bit chilly.

So I gave her a blanket and a lecture about the high price of heating oil, and asked her to stop the shenanigans. The thermostat has remained turned off ever since.

My First Spirit Board: Chris' Story

The old 1980s commercial for the Ouija board game posed the question: *It's only a game. Isn't it?*

Even today, more than 100 years after Ouija was first commercially produced, the debate continues over whether a simple board game can be a tool for evil. A running argument among those who research the paranormal is that these boards open doors and windows unlike other forms of spirit communication. Some claim they invite darker forces like demons into the real world; most think they are a harmless toy, used by teenagers at slumber parties to try to scare themselves. How can something sold next to Don't Spill the Beans be a path to the devil himself, inviting the people who use it to lose their souls? Would Wal-Mart, which won't even carry a hip-hop CD with profane lyrics, really sell a witchboard in its toy department?

The majority of people who use a Ouija game—especially those who use them for fun—will never encounter anything. There are, however, those stories that pop up, making you wonder whether the board is a magnet for activity or a focal point for people who are already experiencing the paranormal.

Every talking board has a story, usually involving wacky things that happened while people were using it. I have marveled at the stories people have told me over the years. Most are insignificant moments of unexplained activity, like a light flickering or a spirit knowing too much about the people using the board. These instances can be explained away.

Then there are the more disturbing and less frequent occurrences, like the time a board told a group of girls someone dangerous was outside, only to have the prowlers caught a few minutes later. Many of the stories focus on the boards becoming an obsession to the users, who tell of using them every night for a week at a time, or spending days researching something the board told them. They range from simple stories of overuse to one story I was told about a college student who became so obsessed after playing, he spent all his free time making boards out of anything he could find.

These tales paint the board with a similar brush. An average person starts to play

How can something sold next to Don't Spill the Beans be a path to the devil himself, inviting the people who use it to lose their souls?

The board is not a way to communicate with the haunting: the board is the haunting.

with one, usually as part of a group, and then something happens. The common theme is that the board acts as a trigger to the activity, but the activity is more about the board than the ghost itself. Several ghosts seem to come into the user's life over a short period of time, and only by getting rid of the board does the activity stop. The board is not a way to communicate with the haunting: the board *is* the haunting.

Looking back, I am not sure when my first board became haunted. It was used for years with no negative activity. My parents kept it in the linen closet and every once in a while took it out for laughs. I was certain it was more powerful than others because it had come from Salem, Massachusetts, home of the infamous witch trials. Years later, I discovered most Ouija boards had a similar label, although few modern-day boards are actually produced there.

The trouble seems to have started when an old girlfriend of my mine, who practiced witchcraft, conducted a special ritual blessing the board and preparing it for our use. The fact that we were using it in one of most haunted buildings in Boston, the old Charlesgate Hotel, made us believe the things we experienced there were due to the location, not the board.

The night of the ritual, we used the board and contacted a spirit that said it was an old sorcerer. I allowed the spirit to try to channel through me, and an hour later I had to be restrained as I tried to choke myself. We felt the whole incident was a case of overactive imaginations, too little sleep, and intention impacting reality. We continued to use the board, although the woman who had blessed it refused to ever put her hands on the planchette again.

We used the board frequently over the next few months, always getting more responses and having more odd things happen than most other people. One of our strangest experiences has become part of the lore of the building and is still told on ghost tours through the city.

A spirit who referred to itself as Federal Government took over the board and demanded we talk to it while we were trying to communicate with other spirits. Over a long period of time, unexplained things happened in our room—items went missing, radios and alarms went off and on, and dark figures were seen out of the corners of our eyes. My girlfriend refused to enter the room.

The whole situation centered on my roommate, a womanizer who the spirit was determined to kill because he treated woman badly. It seemed ridiculous when viewed logically, but there were too many coincidences for us to ignore. We kept using the board through it all, and Federal Government kept communicating with us.

One time while we were using the board, my roommate was in the shower. As Federal Government pushed the other spirit we were speaking to off the board, running over the words ACDC over and over again, my roommate watched as the lights went out above him. His first instinct was to screw the light bulb back in—an unwise idea, as he was covered in water.

A short time later, an ex-girlfriend with whom he had a destructive relationship, confirmed our suspicions that whatever Federal Government was, it was not to be taken lightly. A spirit with the same name had contacted her years earlier, claiming to be a

One of several variations of Ouija, or spirit, boards.

demon. The spirit said it would kill anyone who wronged her or interfered with its relationship with her.

I always assumed it was the ghosts we came into contact with that caused the chaos and the board was just a background piece in the story, not the main character. That changed when I moved out of the dormitory and into an apartment with a friend for the summer.

We rarely used the Ouija board, but whenever we did, it dominated our lives for a few days. Our conversations revolved around it, and we spent most nights hunched over it, trying to make sense of the random letters it pointed to. Then, for whatever reason, we stopped using and talking about it, and stored it in a closet. But the board would not leave me alone.

The night of the ritual, we used the board and contacted a spirit that said it was an old sorcerer. I allowed the spirit to try to channel through me, and an hour later I had to be restrained as I tried to choke myself.

I started having nightmares almost every night. Each dream started with me involved in a normal daytime activity, and then it would change. In one, I was preparing food at the deli where I worked. A wind began blowing all of the equipment and containers around, breaking glass around the restaurant. Spiders came pouring out of the refrigerators and freezers, covering my legs. An unseen hand cut the woman I worked with, and she turned to me, crying, "You have to use the board and get them to stop." I woke up and the board was on the floor next to me, the planchette on top of the smiling sun symbol.

All of the nightmares followed the same pattern. I was walking the streets of Boston in one, and people started to chase me. Someone said they would give me shelter, but I had to use the board. In another, a beautiful woman and I were kissing, and she suggested we use the board before we made love. After each dream, I woke up to see the board either out of storage, or the door to the closet, where it was stored, standing open.

These weird dreams and unusual activities fed my enthusiasm for the paranormal. It was 1995 and I had already started documenting paranormal activity and investigating haunted sites. I began to wonder if the board itself contained something unreal and dark. Using it wasn't as fun as it used to be. Instead, the board acted like a jealous lover, unable to deal with the fact that I had moved on.

It was not only during nightmares that the board tried to press itself back into my life. Although we lived in a studio apartment, my roommate and I did not see much of each other. We were both working long hours, and she had a new boyfriend with his own place. However, we both felt a heaviness in the room whenever we entered it, and at night we often felt we were being watched.

One time I came home to find the Ouija board in the middle of the room. That in itself didn't raise an eyebrow—it was becoming a regular occurrence. Hovering over the board, however, spinning around and forming a tornado-like cone, were dozens of flies. I tried to swat them away, but they wouldn't leave until I returned the board to the closet.

Another time I had some female friends over. They insisted we play with the board and I hesitantly agreed. We took it out and spoke to several different spirits. I was impressed by how powerfully the spirits came through and how clear their messages were.

It grew late, so I agreed to walk the women to their car, but the apartment door refused to open. The

In my head, I heard a voice say my name. It then said, "You will use it or I'll kill your whole family."

lock was jammed in one position. The planchette, which we had returned to the box, was now sitting on the "No" corner of the board. I moved it down to "Goodbye," and we heard the lock click. The door opened slightly and the women ran through, saying I didn't have to walk out with them.

I left the board out and went to bed. A few hours later, my roommate and I were jarred from sleep by the fire alarm. The alarm, positioned above the board, was going off even though there was no fire.

My final night with the board pushed me over the edge. A week after the fire alarm incident, I was awakened by a barking dog—extremely odd considering pets were not allowed in our apartment building and the noise seemed to be coming from right inside the room. I propped myself up in bed and saw a dark figure, like a man in an all-black body suit, sitting on my roommate's bed and moving a hand over her as if stroking her body.

In my head, I heard a voice say my name. It then said, "You will use it or I'll kill your whole family." At that moment, the closet door slowly opened and the board fell off the top shelf. When I looked back at my roommate's bed, the dark figure was gone.

I got the board, ran out the door, and threw it into the dumpster behind the building. I ignored the pounding on the metal as I walked back to the front door. I had no desire to see it ever again.

The decapitated body of a foreign woman was found in the same dumpster a few weeks later. Some police friends not involved in the investigation told me they were recommending I be put on the short list of suspects because it was the second time in as many years a body had been dumped on a property where I was a resident. I laughed it off because it was so absurd.

Although I have used many other Ouija boards over the years, I have never felt the same intimidation or heaviness as I did while using that first board. Logic tells me the Ouija board had no connection to the murder, but there is a tiny voice that always questions the possibility and makes me pause.

Sarah Finds a Board

It is rare to find anyone who has actually purchased an Ouija or spirit board. Boards usually just seem to "be there," perhaps owned by a longtime family member or picked up at a long-ago yard sale. Ask people where they got their boards and they will usually shrug their shoulders. They have no memory of the acquisition.

Boards seem to be one of the last true artifacts handed down from generation to generation. You can visit the board game aisle of the local toy store to find a new glow-in-the-dark version or you can buy one at your local occult dealer, but the casual user won't do either. Instead, spirit boards are discovered in the attic or basement of parents' or grandparents' houses, under a tattered quilt, on top of old books, or next to the old game of Operation with the funny bone long lost.

People take boards out of storage and breathe new life into them, sometimes asking the former owner if any paranormal activity occurred when they used it, but more often not knowing its history. Many people associated with the paranormal condemn any use of the spirit board because of this kind of "blind" communication, which is like walking along a dark street in the worst part of town, tempting fate. For others, not knowing a board's history is part of the thrill.

Sarah knows the history of her board and the colorful path it took to her is as interesting as the events she witnessed with it. She now admits the unusual things she experienced with it may be linked to the road it traveled to get to her, although part of her wonders if the board itself caused some of the sad things it saw.

Sarah's board was made in the 1930s and belonged to her great aunt, who lived on a farm with her brother and sister. While she is unsure of any communication they might have gotten from it, there was tragedy linked to it in those early days.

A fire broke out in the barn where her great aunt kept the board. Several of the animals were burned alive, and the damage to the barn was so severe, the family had

Many people associated with the paranormal condemn any use of the spirit board because of this kind of "blind" communication, which is like walking along a dark street in the worst part of town, tempting fate.

> Once they talked to a spirit claiming to be Marie Antoinette, who spelled out, "I want your head." As the young girls laughed, a book fell on her friend's neck.

to tear it down and build a new one. Almost all of the family's possessions stored in the barn were lost, but the spirit board was untouched. It was found on a burnt railing, with not a mark on it.

When Sarah's aunt left the farm, she took the board with her. Years later, it ended up with Sarah's grandmother, who didn't use it. Sarah found it while cleaning her grandmother's house. She may have been young at the time, but she recognized what it was and how it was used. Her story is typical: Most people cannot remember the first time they used a board, and the understanding of how it is used seems instinctive.

When Sarah got a little older, she would take the board out when she was with her friends or during sleepovers. She had many experiences while using it, often harmless or amusing incidents when viewed by themselves. Once, they talked to a spirit claiming to be Marie Antoinette, who spelled out, "I want your head." As the young girls laughed, a book fell on her friend's neck.

Sarah brought the board to the home of another friend, who thought she lived in a haunted house. For a while, they talked to "nice" spirits before something else communicated with them. It spelled out, "DIE, DIE, DIE," and the temperature in the room dropped. They tried to move the planchette to "Goodbye," but it wouldn't move. The lights turned on and off and furniture began to move. Sarah's friend felt cold hands on her neck and began to scream. Sarah threw the board against the wall and everything stopped.

Things got more intense when Sarah moved out of the house. In her second year of college, she returned home to get some furniture and personal belongings because she was moving off-campus into an apartment with some friends. The board was on the washing machine in the basement, although later her mother said she had not seen it in years.

Sarah took the board with her and began to notice odd things almost immediately.

"I could not keep things alive near that thing," she said. "We kept it in the living room because we would use it when friends came over. All

For a while they talked to "nice" spirits before something else communicated with them. It spelled out, "DIE, DIE, DIE," and the temperature in the room dropped.

the plants died. I thought it was weird, but my roommates didn't notice. I took it into my room and put it under my bed. The fish I kept on my bureau died the next day."

There was something compelling her to keep the board, which is another trait commonly found in people who spend time using it. A friend who practiced Wicca blessed the board and the scary sessions stopped, but ironically, this led to some disappointment.

"It didn't seem to work as well. We would talk to people, but there was nothing that raised the hairs on the back of our necks. We missed being scared of it," Sarah said.

That changed the night she woke up and saw an old man in her room using the board. He was bald and wrinkled and sitting cross-legged on the floor in the moonlight coming through her window. She could almost see through him, and she knew he was a ghost. He motioned for her to come over and it was then she noticed that in front of him was the board, which she had put away in the closet a few days earlier.

"I screamed and when my roommates came in and turned on the light, he disappeared. Maybe it was the end of a dream, but the board was still there on the floor," she said. "I threw it in the dumpster. There was something evil about that old man, so let him go haunt the dump. That board is where it belongs."

Sarah, now entering her forties, has not used a board since. When people take one out at parties or get-togethers, she finds a reason to leave the room. Sometimes history is meant to stay in the past.

Section Five

HAUNTINGS
AROUND
THE HOUSE

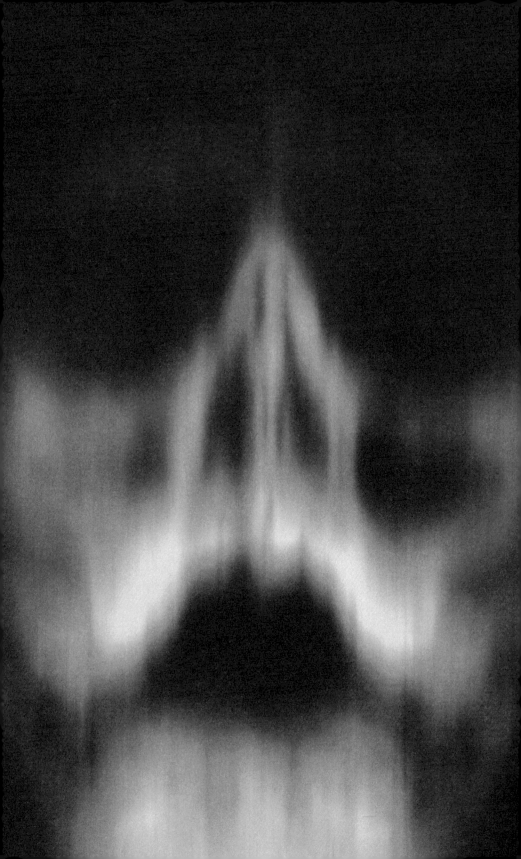

Bed of Dread

When a person is terrified by something in the night, the best remedy is usually to crawl under the covers and hide there until it either goes away or the sun comes up. But what happens when it's the *bed* that is so terrifying?

Caesar related the story about a family he knew that purchased a home that came with a bed frame. The family's son decided to use it, and from the moment he began sleeping in the bed, strange things occurred. Lights and other electrical devices would turn on and off on their own, and inexplicable shadows would flicker on the walls. Bed sheets and blankets would be pulled off or even float above the bed, and the son would often have nightmares and wake up to bitter cold temperatures and a feeling of being watched.

At first, only the son endured these hellish, sleepless nights. He finally told his father, but his father didn't believe him. He thought it was his son's imagination, which would calm down once he got used to the new house. But after constant pestering from his son, the father finally decided to spend a few nights in the boy's room, just to prove that nothing was actually happening. It didn't take long before the strange incidents happened to him as well, and he, too, became a believer.

The family decided to do a little more research on the history of the home and discovered that someone had committed suicide in the house. While there was no proof that the bed or even the room it was in had belonged to the suicide victim, it still hit a little too close to home for the family. They got rid of the bed frame and soon after, everything returned to normal.

When a person is terrified by something in the night, the best remedy is usually to crawl under the covers and hide there until it either goes away or the sun comes up. But what happens when it's the bed that is so terrifying?

Altered Belief

As a paranormal researcher for many years, John Brightman is used to dealing with family drama when investigating private residences. He's also used to dealing with haunted objects and even a few allegedly cursed ones, but never before have all three situations combined into one strange case that still leaves him wondering exactly what happened.

Author's note: All the family names have been changed.

Lucy called John's group, New England Paranormal Research, to help her deal with paranormal activity that was going on in the house where her mother, sister, and brother had all lived. All three had recently died, and various phenomena had been taking place in the house: objects moving around, doors opening and closing on their own, and other such things. But when her young granddaughter reported seeing her dead uncle near the staircase, and when Lucy herself saw a strange mist coming up from the basement doorway, she knew something was haunting the house and she wanted it gone.

According to Lucy, her older brother, Armand, lived in the house with his mother Mabel. Mabel was in her early 90s and had not been in great health. Then again, neither had Armand; he was in his 60s and he, too, had become ill and was having trouble taking care of Mabel. Also living with them was Armand's sister, Erica, who wasn't doing much to help.

One day, when Armand wasn't at home, Erica saw her chance to speak to her mother alone. Erica told her that if she agreed to sign the house and everything else over to her, she would take care of her and she wouldn't end up in a nursing home if things got too bad with Armand. Mabel agreed to do so because she had a great fear of dying in a nursing home or some other assisted-care facility. She wanted to die in her home, with dignity. She signed everything over to Erica, including all the legal power to decide her care.

When Armand found out, he was furious. He was the one who had remained at home taking care of his elderly mother while Erica went on living her life. According to Brightman, Armand had "gone nuts" from being cooped up with his mother for so long, in combination with his own health issues. He thought he was going to inherit everything when his mother died—his reward for being the dedicated son.

But as it turned out, Erica lied. After Mabel signed everything over to her, Erica put her in a nursing home anyway. Mabel died not long after, and the cause of death was never really determined. Brightman figured it must have been natural causes, but the research his group did suggested that the medical examiner had never made a

Little stickpins had been inserted into the toy in various positions, like a voodoo doll.

solid determination. Both medical and police reports provided no answer.

About two months after Mabel's passing, Erica's spleen ruptured and she died as a result. A few months later, Armand passed away as well. Within about an eight-month span, all three parties involved in the spat had died.

As the only surviving family member, Lucy took possession of the house and began cleaning it out and preparing to place it on the market.

That's when she discovered the altar.

In Armand's room was a small desk with three or four candles placed across its surface. In the center of a desk was a strange box, which Lucy couldn't remember ever seeing before. Before he took ill, her brother was a successful commercial fisherman, and she thought it looked like something he might have come across in his many travels.

The box measured about eight inches long and four inches wide and resembled a jewelry box. Inside was an old and faded stuffed toy that looked like a fish. Tacked to it were photographs of three people, two of whom she instantly recognized—Erica and Mabel. The third picture was of a man she did not recognize. Little stickpins had been inserted into the toy in various positions, like a voodoo doll.

Lucy didn't think her brother was into voodoo. Yes, he was eccentric—if you came to visit without calling first, he'd slam the door in your face, no matter what. He had collected many items related to fishing, like old buoys and netting and other such objects, and arranged them in the backyard in a way that made sense only to him. But voodoo? That went beyond anything she imagined.

Yet as she continued to examine the contents of the wooden box, she found additional items that made it look more like voodoo was the case. There were extra pins, dried herbs that might have been sage, and mysterious oils and ointments with no labels. It looked as if many of the items were old. Perhaps this was something Armand had been practicing for years.

The voodoo experts said the pins were inserted in the right places to inflict pain on the intended targets, but not knowing if the proper chants and prayers were used makes them unsure a curse was activated.

It was possible—a fisherman lives something of a nomadic existence and comes in contact with people from many different cultures. Some of those who work in commercial fishing still bring old world beliefs and traditions on the ships with them.

Armand sailed out of the port of New Bedford, Massachusetts, alongside a great many seamen of Portuguese and Brazilian decent. Within those cultures exists a form of black magic known as macumba, and it is possible Armand learned the magic from one of them. Macumba rituals are often used to seek revenge on family members who have done harm, often utilizing a photograph of that person to do so. For that reason, many superstitious Brazilians will not allow a photograph of themselves to be given to anyone they don't know.

Upon discovering the box and altar, Lucy's first instinct wasn't to call a paranormal investigation team. Instead, she hired a medium to help the restless spirits move from the house and remove bad vibes brought about by any strange rituals her brother was practicing. Another reason she sought help from a psychic was to address rumors of a stash of money hidden somewhere in the house. Armand had been successful in the fishing industry, but there was no trace of his profits anywhere.

The box the doll was found in.

The medium told Lucy that Armand's strange outdoor collection of seafaring memorabilia was some sort of map detailing where he buried his money in the yard, but the family never found any of it. She also explained that the pins that were stuck into the fish doll were arranged in a way that would inflict pain on the intended target. Without knowing about Erica or how she died, she noted that one of the pins appeared to be placed in what would represent the spleen. A shiver went down Lucy's back.

The medium also told Lucy that if they buried the box with the fish doll in the yard, the hauntings would stop. Unfortunately, that didn't turn out to be true, which was how John Brightman and NEPR got involved.

"It was just a weird situation," John said. "(Lucy) called us in and explained the whole situation with her brother, sister, and mother. We investigated one night for over nine hours, and we captured absolutely nothing in terms of evidence."

Perhaps the haunting was meant only for the family to experience.

"It was kind of a let-down," he said. "I was hoping to get something that would back up what they were saying."

John and his team even dug up the box with the fish doll inside, which at that point had been buried for about three months. They returned it to the house and attempted to use it as a "trigger object," hoping that it would stir up activity again.

"Again, nothing," he said.

John took pictures of the box and the doll and sent them to colleagues who are

The doll that may have held a curse.

authorities on voodoo. The voodoo experts said the pins were inserted in the right places to inflict pain on the intended targets, but not knowing if Armand invoked the proper chants and prayers makes them unsure that he "activated" the curse.

Was Armand really so upset with his sister and mother for the sneaky arrangements they made behind his back that he put a macumba curse on them, leading to their deaths? And did his evil actions result in his own passing as well?

One mystery that still remains is the identity of the man in the third photograph stuck to the fish doll. Speculation is that it could have been a fishing partner who wronged Armand in some way. Perhaps a deal gone bad is the reason Armand's money has never been found, and he turned to macumba to seek his revenge on his partner as well as his family. That might even explain why the doll was in the shape of a fish.

When the box was removed from the property, all the strange activity came to an abrupt end, and a sense of peace that had been missing for many decades once again filled its rooms.

The box is now in Brightman's possession. He plans to eventually give it to John Zaffis, paranormal investigator and collector of haunted objects, to be placed in his museum, John Zaffis Museum of the Paranormal.

Brightman believes Armand's spirit perhaps felt guilty about the pain he had inflicted on his loved ones and realized he was wrong to be so upset. Once the box and the doll were removed, his spirit was able to find peace and move on to be reunited with his mother and sister, where all would be forgiven.

The Haunted
Travel Clock

When Richard was a child, his mother owned a small wind-up travel clock that had been a gift from her grandmother. Richard never felt comfortable around the clock, saying it always gave him the creeps, even though he had no idea why. He said it looked like a small version of the famous "Big Ben" clock in London. It had a gold case and a green face with Roman numerals in a gold color. The hands and wind-up key were brass.

Although it was an ordinary little clock, it just never sat right with Richard. Just being in the same room with it would give him fits of paranoia, as if it was ticking down the minutes of his life.

When Richard's great-grandmother died, the clock stopped working. No matter what was tried, it wouldn't start up again. Richard began to wonder if maybe the tick-tocks hadn't been measuring his life, but rather that of his great-grandmother. The thought was enough to send shivers down his spine.

Richard's mother never threw the broken clock away because it held sentimental value for her, and every time he looked at it, he would get a sick feeling in the pit of his stomach. When his mother was out one day, Richard buried the clock in the backyard. He said there was "merry hell" when his mother found the clock was missing, but she never discovered what he did with it.

But even now—more than 30 years after he moved away from the buried haunted clock—Richard can still see its green face and brass hands in his sleep, and hear its crazed second hand ticking away in the night.

Just being in the same room with the clock would give him fits of paranoia, as if it was ticking down the minutes of his life.

The Haunted Butter Dish

One morning Heather was making toast for her two children. She put the butter dish, which had been given to her by her grandmother, on the island countertop in her kitchen, and turned her back for a moment to put the bread in the toaster. When she turned around to get the butter dish, it had disappeared.

"I asked the kids if they took it, even though I knew they hadn't because they had been in the living room watching television," Heather said. "I remember yelling out loud, 'This is stupid. Who loses a butter dish?' "

Without the butter, Heather decided she'd have to make something else for breakfast instead. As she went to throw the toast in the trash, she looked back at the kitchen island and the butter dish had reappeared—right where she had left it.

Heather didn't think much of the disappearing butter dish until it happened to her husband as well. One morning he made toast as Heather played with the children in the living room. When he reached for the butter dish, he saw it had disappeared from the kitchen island. He called out to Heather to see if she had moved it.

"I told him to just give it a minute and it would come back," Heather said. "At first he said, 'Yeah, right,' but when he looked down again, it was there again. I told him it was just haunted and he had to deal with it."

That was four years ago, and the butter dish still has a tendency to disappear and reappear. Although there has been ghostly activity in her home, the butter dish seems to be the focus of the haunting.

Heather didn't think much of the disappearing butter dish until it happened to her husband as well.

The disappearing and reappearing butter dish.

Don't Sit There!

On display at the Thirsk Museum in North Yorkshire, England, is the famous Busby Stoop Chair, said to be about 300 years old. Nobody has sat in the chair since 1978, and with good reason—the chair is allegedly cursed and responsible for at least three deaths.

The story goes something like this: There was a man named Thomas Busby, who owned the Busby Stoop Inn just outside of North Yorkshire. He was married to the daughter of Daniel Awety, with whom Busby was involved in some illicit, illegal activities. One of their crimes, known as "coin clipping," involved shaving off parts of coins in order to create enough metal to forge their own counterfeit coins.

In 1702, Awety and Busby got into an argument, supposedly over their criminal enterprise, and Busby stormed off. The next time he saw his father-in-law was in the pub, sitting in Busby's favorite chair, supposedly to taunt Busby. Enraged, Busby threw him out of his pub. A short time later and likely full of ale—Busby was a notorious drunkard—he snuck into Awety's home, bludgeoned him to death with a hammer, and stashed his body in the woods.

The body was found and Busby was, of course, the main suspect. He was arrested at the pub and dragged down the main street to the gallows. Along the way, he shouted out a curse that anybody else who dared to sit in his favorite chair would die just as cruelly as Awety had, and as Busby soon would.

He may have just made good on that curse.

The chair has been loosely linked to a handful of deaths in the past few centuries. A chimney sweep who sat in it in the late 1800s was found dead the next morning, hanging from a gatepost near where Busby himself was hanged.

During World War II, visiting airmen would sit in the chair, and their entire squadron would perish. Two particular pilots were killed before they even got the chance to fly again, when their car crashed into a tree on their way back to the airbase. Heart attacks, car wrecks, and other terrible afflictions often befell whoever sat in the chair, and the legend of its curse began to spread throughout England.

Soon, the chair became sort of a "Bloody Mary" to pub-goers, a challenge to show

As Busby was dragged down the main street to the gallows, he shouted out a curse that anybody else who dared to sit in his favorite chair would die cruelly.

that you were not afraid of it. People would dare one another to sit in it, often resulting in fatal consequences. The last straw came in the 1970s, when a young man who sat in it on a dare fell to his death while working on a roof. After that, the chair was placed in the basement, presumably to prevent anyone from sitting in it again. That is, until a delivery man decided to take a break in it one morning—and afterward, just a few miles down the road, his truck crashed and he was killed.

At that point, the owner of the pub donated the chair to the Thirsk Museum. No one has been allowed to sit in it since.

Don't Sit There, Either!

Among the ornate architecture and mesmerizing landscapes of the famed mansions of Newport, Rhode Island, is the rather unique Belcourt Castle. It was built between 1891 and 1894 as a 60-room "summer cottage" for Oliver Hazard Perry Belmont, who built the Louis XIII-style mansion for $3 million.

Belcourt Castle remained in the Belmont family until 1940. It went through a series of owners and saw continued neglect until the Tinney family purchased it in 1956. The Tinneys spent many years restoring the castle to its former glory, filling it with antique furnishings from around the world—and with them, a whole slew of ghosts.

There were no real reports of Belcourt Castle being haunted before the arrival of all those antiques, but these days there are so many ghosts, current owner Harle Hope Hanson Tinney actually conducts ghost tours of her home.

Although more than a few objects in Belcourt Castle are known for their associated spirit attachments, none are more famous than the two chairs in the French Gothic Ballroom.

Most visitors to the castle describe a severe drop in room temperature surrounding the two chairs; no matter what season it is, the air surrounding them is always ice cold. While the spirits surrounding the chairs are both adamant about not wanting anyone to sit in them, they do so through two different methods. One chair simply cannot be sat in; there is a force of resistance so great it's like a force field around it. The other chair can be sat in, but if you sit in it you will soon be tossed out.

What could be the nature of the ghosts that haunt these chairs? Why do they remain, for lack of a better term, glued to their seats? Perhaps these chairs hold special significance to the spirits, and they have no desire to share them with tour-goers and visitors to Belcourt Castle. Or maybe there are so many ghosts roaming the hallowed halls that these spirits had to claim at least one spot for themselves.

Section Six

HAUNTED JEWELRY

The Healing Medal

Everett and his wife were worried when their seven-year-old son, Logun, began acting strange for brief periods of time. When they took him to a doctor, he was diagnosed with localized focal seizures. Logun was scheduled to have an MRI in order to rule out lesions, tumors, or cancer as the culprit of these seizures.

As the test loomed closer, Everett found himself in a panic over what the doctors might find. On one hand, he wanted to know what was wrong with his young son, but on the other, he was afraid of what they would find. Why was this happening? What kind of bad news were they going to get next?

Two days before Logun's test, Everett was fumbling with the change in his pocket. He reached down deep and felt something strange mixed in among the coins. He pulled it out, realizing it was a pendant of some kind. When he looked closer, he saw it was a St. Christopher's medal. Everett had never owned such a medal, nor had he ever seen one before.

St. Christopher is believed to offer safety from sudden death, and travelers often wear his medal. Some medals are accompanied by variations of the phrases, "Look upon St. Christopher and go on reassured" or "If you trust in St. Christopher, no harm will befall you." It is also thought that St. Christopher will protect believers from pestilence, which we now recognize as infectious disease.

The day of Logun's test was difficult to endure. The MRI took twice as long as it should have because the doctors needed extra imaging to try to locate the root of the boy's affliction. Everett kept reaching into his pocket and holding the medal between his fingers, figuring

The St. Christopher medal.

its mysterious appearance was some sort of sign.

The next day, Logun's test results brought wonderful news. He was in the rare but lucky three percent of people who have focal seizures but no abnormal growths or cancer as the cause. Anti-seizure medication would correct everything.

Everett began to think that the St. Christopher medal was lucky or perhaps even blessed, and decided he would put it on a necklace for his son. But when he reached into his pocket, the medal was gone. He searched for three days but couldn't locate it. He started to think that perhaps it had gone on to help another family that needed it, appearing out of nowhere just as it had for him.

About a month and a half later, Everett was scheduled to have knee surgery. The day before his surgery, he found the St. Christopher medal lying in the driveway of his home, right by the driver's side door of his car. Even if he had dropped it following Logun's test, he surely would have spotted it in the six weeks since that time.

Everett felt the medal reappeared to help him through his surgery and it did just that, until the day he got his stitches removed—when it vanished again.

Everett kept reaching into his pocket and holding the medal between his fingers, figuring its mysterious appearance was some sort of sign.

An Assurance From the Unknown

Sometimes the paranormal aspects of a haunted item stem from how the item is obtained, rather than from how it behaves after it is acquired. Objects can appear out of nowhere, finding their way into the hands of a person who needs them.

For centuries, people have reported odd items appearing out of thin air. When the item is something you need at that time, it's hard to deny that there is a special kind of force at work, and when the delivery man can't be used to explain as to why an item suddenly appears, it becomes an even deeper mystery.

Jenna isn't sure whether the people she saw that night in 1991—and the man who seemed to lead them—were ghosts or angels. She and a friend, who also saw them, tend to base their ghostly appearance on religious beliefs or what they think about the paranormal.

"I have no idea who those people were," Jenna said, thinking back on it 20 years later. "And honestly, I sometimes question if they were even people and not guardian angels, not that I even really believe in that. But it was so odd."

Both Jenna and her friend have had other paranormal experiences, and one thing they agree on is that at no time did the leader seem entirely human, even if what he gave them was real—a simple marble.

It all started when their small group of friends went through an AIDS scare.

"I was 16, and the AIDS crisis was in full swing. PSAs (public service announcements) were everywhere, telling us all to get tested right away," Jenna said. "I had just started having sex a few months before this, and being a good girl, I decided to do as I was told. I was terrified to get the test. Even though I had only had one partner and we used protection, I was convinced that I was probably going to be punished by some higher power for having sex before marriage."

While no one in Jenna's crowd was promiscuous, they were scared. Several people in their community had been exposed to the disease. Jenna, already a bit of a hypochondriac, was the first to be tested. Something in her heart told her she would not like the results.

"I went and did it anyway. My friend, Amy, came with me, and after it was over we decided to go out to eat at Applebee's. It was not a place I really ever went, and I have no idea why we decided to go that evening. But I needed to vent my fears and it was a place

The ghosts appeared out of nowhere under one of the streetlights that glowed in the parking lot.

The marble was unremarkable, but holding it, Jenna was overcome with a sense of peace and the feeling that, as the mysterious stranger had predicted, everything was going to be okay.

for us to go, away from our parents, and talk about it all."

It was late, and most of the people in the restaurant were teens. The ghosts appeared out of nowhere under one of the streetlights that glowed in the parking lot. One second the lot was empty, and the next there were four teens making their way across the pavement, too far away from anything to have walked up unseen.

"I definitely remember there was a guy walking out in front, with longish brown hair, probably in his 20s. I had never seen any of them before," Jenna said.

The leader was handsome and well dressed in jeans, a button-down shirt, and sports jacket too thick for the hot Dallas weather. His whole appearance was clean and attractive. Jenna remembers being as arrested by his natty looks as by his sudden materialization.

There was also a light around him Jenna can't, even to this day, fully describe. He was illuminated by the streetlight above him, but there was also light that seemed to come from behind him. Jenna, who had studied auras, is reluctant to say he was glowing.

"It's more he was bathed in light," she said.

The vision looked at her as if nothing else existed in the world, his face serene. He wasn't smiling so much as simply looking peaceful.

Although Jenna's friend, Amy, was facing the window, she hadn't spotted the mysterious people yet. Jenna stopped their conversation so that Amy might notice them out the window, but by that time they had entered the restaurant. They seemed to disappear from the parking lot and reappear by the door in the blink of an eye. It was obvious they hadn't run the distance because they remained calm and graceful. The leader of the group was unrumpled, his hair and clothes still in perfect order. More importantly, as he opened the door and walked in, no one noticed he was there.

"They came right into the restaurant. They walked directly up to Amy and me," Jenna said. They didn't stop to talk to anyone, and Jenna doesn't remember anyone looking at them. "The guy in the front looked right at me and said, 'Hold out your hand.' I looked at him, but did not speak, and I put my hand out. He placed his hand over mine and put something in it, but did not take his hand away, right away. He looked at me and said, 'Everything is going to be all right.' Then he closed my hand up so that I could not see what he put inside, and he and the others turned around and left. They did not eat, they did not get drinks, nothing."

For a moment, Jenna and Amy were too stunned to move. "I opened my hand and inside was a beautiful cat's eye marble," Jenna said. "I knew, looking at it, that this was a sign that I was going to be all right, that I did not have AIDS."

The marble was unremarkable, but holding it, Jenna was overcome with a sense of peace and the feeling that, as the mysterious stranger had predicted, everything was going to be okay.

Jenna and Amy got up to follow the ghostly people, but they had vanished again. They questioned the hostess, but she had never even seen them come in.

Jenna's test was negative, and she passed the marble to the next person who went in for the test.

"Amy and I made a pact to pass the marble on to anyone we knew who was getting the test. So I gave it to her when it was her turn, and I suppose she passed it on."

The marble made its way through their group, one by one, bringing tranquility to whoever possessed it at the moment. It was like a security blanket, giving peace of mind. But before long it disappeared, and no one could quite remember who had it last. No ghostly young man appeared to take the marble away, and no exploding spectral entity destroyed it. It was just not needed anymore and vanished.

What happened that night is not easy to explain. The marble itself didn't cause Jenna and Amy to see visions. Many parts of the story, from the mysterious group of people to the calm each person felt, make a sort of sense when looked at individually. What happens, though, when all these elements combine into one paranormal experience?

"It was probably one of the strangest, most wonderful things that has ever happened to me. I will never forget it," Jenna said.

But don't tell them that what they witnessed was not a ghost. They know there are times when you just have to believe your eyes.

The marble made its way through their group, one by one, bringing tranquility to whomever possessed it at the moment.

I Dream of Djinn

The ring's significance in societies around the world is undeniable, and its symbolism reflects the culture of the person wearing it. In most Western countries, the ring is a token of one's commitment to another person. Wedding rings are thought to connect directly to the heart, claddagh rings show if you are single or involved with someone special, and mood rings tell others how you're feeling.

The ring's special meanings can range from eternity, due to its physical design of the endless circle, to magic, as in J. R. R. Tolkien's *Lord of the Rings*. It may also send a cultural message or show prosperity or status.

There are countless stories of haunted rings. Because of their close personal relationships with the wearers, they are often the focus of spirits that are looking to communicate with the people left behind. That means the young woman who finds the ring her deceased grandmother was buried wearing can find peace with the dead.

The Edwards brothers didn't have such good luck. Some might say they were doomed from the beginning. Haunted rings are supposed to be inherited, not bought through an online auction.

Brian and Ray Jay had been investigating the paranormal for a bit when they decided to get more personally involved in a haunting. They'd been interested in looking for ghosts for years, and those first few investigations fueled their desire.

"After a few paranormal investigations," said Ray Jay, "Brian decided he wanted to learn more about 'haunted items.' He found some rings on eBay purported to be haunted. The one he decided to purchase said it had a djinn attached to it. If I remember correctly, it was supposed to be a guardian djinn or something. It was advertised as a positive entity."

Some of the most common haunted items for sale online are rings that have a djinn, or jinn, attached to them. What we know about djinns is based mainly on old literature, although every week newspapers from the Middle East or from parts of Africa post stories of people cursed by them, falling victim to horrible tragedies or being blamed for crimes.

> Because of their close personal relationships with the wearers, rings are often the focus of spirits that are looking to communicate with the people left behind.

The word "djinn" is the basis of the word genie, but djinns have little to do with beautiful women trapped in lamps. In the West we recognize them from romantic legends such as *The Arabian Nights*, but they have been part of a strong belief system for thousands of years. While there is a kind of neutral supreme level of djinns, most seem to fall into a limbo realm. Some are helpful and can be called on in times of need; others are malicious, demon-like creatures that can cause great suffering when awakened.

According to the mythology surrounding them, they are often trapped in objects, and people can conjure them or fall victim to them depending on the type of djinn. When used to stir up trouble, the old rule of the witches often applies: What you send out comes back to you threefold. While their traditional imprisonment is in the lamp, modern theories hold that anything can be used to contain them. When it comes to demons for sale, rings are the best buy.

As often happens when you dabble in things you don't understand, the supernatural has a mind of its own.

"On Aug. 14, 2009, Brian found a ring advertised to be haunted by a djinn/genie," Ray Jay remembered. "He purchased it for $9.85, plus shipping, from an eBay seller. The exact name of the item, according to his PayPal account, [was] 'Haunted Powerful Ilmu Khodam Spirit Djinn Genie' ring."

"Ilmu Khodam" has many meanings to people who study magic. There is a form called conjuring, or necro-slavery, practiced by some. Where djinns are

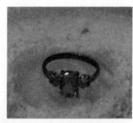

The ring with a djinn spirit attached to it.

prominent, Ilmu Khodam means a way for practitioners to raise the spirit of djinn and use it to get what they want. That often means causing pain to or taking control of others. Paranormal theories say this curse or negative energy might remain after the hapless practitioner is no longer working his magic.

"The instructions that came with the ring told the new owner to light a candle and meditate with the ring, inviting the new owner to make friends with the djinn attached to it. So Brian lit a white candle and meditated with the ring, inviting the guardian djinn to be friends.

"The ring was made for a woman's finger, so Brian couldn't put it on, but he took EMF readings of the ring, took pictures of it, and conducted an EVP session with it. He got no results at all—not so much as a dust orb

Haunted items have a habit of breaking the rules.

in a photograph. He also e-mailed the seller, asking about the previous owner of the ring, but got no response back."

Things did not go as the brothers planned. It's sometimes a gamble to buy items online, but the stakes are higher when you're shopping for the paranormal. Your new purchase might be a complete dud and you might live a long and happy life, though this is rare in the world of online ghosts. As often happens when you dabble in things you don't understand, the supernatural had a mind of its own for the brothers.

Not long after Brian had the ring, he experienced a run of bad luck.

"Over the course of the next three to four weeks, Brian's luck seemed to worsen inexplicably. Our living room TV stopped working, the communal PC, the best one in the house at that time, died, and the 'check engine' light in Brian's car came on and could not be deactivated," Ray Jay said. "On top of these things, perhaps related, perhaps not, Brian was meditating one day when an image popped into his mind of a silhouette of his hand, and it was surrounded by this red glow. It didn't feel like a reassuring image." The brothers were amazed by all of this unusual activity.

Many investigators rely on new scientific methods to study the paranormal, to confirm whether or not ghosts exist. The ring rang no paranormal bells.

"Now, when we investigate the paranormal, we rely on verifiable facts, and a random string of unfortunate events, combined with a random mental image, is clearly nowhere close to evidence of paranormal activity. To this day, Brian considers the story of his 'haunted' ring a non-story—not one shred of empirical data to link his 'bad luck' with

Not all djinns are helpful in times of need. Some are malicious demons hellbent on causing great suffering to those who unleash them, as depicted in the horror movie, *Wishmaster*.

the ring, which is too small for him to wear."

A protective circle of sea salt surrounds the ring.

But not all supernatural activity can be explained away. When asked if Brian puts any faith in a haunted or cursed ring, Ray Jay was hesitant to answer. "He is still undecided," he said. "Neither of us is comfortable declaring this ring to truly be 'haunted.' It's a coincidental string of bad luck, coupled with a random mental image that popped up once right after he closed his eyes, when our brains always throw up random images and colors."

Regardless of his words, Brian's actions lean toward superstition. "One day Brian informed me that he bought some sea salt, and I'm welcome to as much of it as I like," Ray Jay said. "And then he tells me why he bought it. He points out that the computer, his car, the TV all happened after he received the ring. Unfortunate things happen and often happen in succession, but it just sort of seemed that they were happening a lot more lately. So Brian decided to surround the ring within a protective circle of salt (he had read that sea salt is supposed to be a better conductor for subtle energies than regular salt) and see if the bad luck stopped.

"About a month or so later, I noticed the ring: It was still on a kitchen counter and still encircled by sea salt," Ray Jay said. "I asked him if he now thought the misfortunes had been caused by the ring. Brian hadn't won the lottery or anything, and at that time he was really undecided as to whether the ring had caused the string of bad luck or if it had just been coincidence. But neither of us has broken the protective circle around it, either."

It has been three years since the ring was surrounded by salt, and no new supernatural activity has occurred since then. The Edwards continue to study the paranormal, keeping ghosts at arm's length, and collecting EVPs and EMF readings. The paranormal is a bit easier to understand that way. It becomes less manageable when spirits have the ability to control and influence your life. Haunted items have a habit of breaking the rules.

For Ray Jay, the mystery of the ring might not make a good tale, mainly because it doesn't sound like a traditional ghost story.

"I guess you could look at it as a paranormal investigator buys a haunted ring to study, then after a really inconvenient run of bad luck, he takes off the ring and is no longer interested in studying haunted objects."

Rocks of Love

Alyssa had been ill for quite some time. During hospital visits, she met another young woman named Erica, who shared the same disease. They were close in age and had so much in common they became nearly inseparable. Alyssa was heartbroken when her friend took a turn for the worse and died unexpectedly.

One of Alyssa's hobbies was creating beaded jewelry, which kept her mind off the physical pain of her illness and the emotional pain of her loss.

One day not long after her friend's death, Alyssa went into her bead drawer and found an amethyst stone, one of her favorites. It was too wide and thick to be used for jewelry, so it shouldn't have been in the drawer. In fact, Alyssa couldn't remember putting it there in the first place. Perfectly heart shaped, the amethyst seemed like a message of love when she needed it most.

Soon after, whenever she was downhearted or when her illness intensified, she would find smooth heart-shaped stones in various places. One might appear in her bead drawer, like the amethyst, or under her pillow.

Alyssa believes Erica is looking down on her and sending her these stones to remind her of the strength of their friendship, even though one of them has passed on to a place where pain and illness do not exist.

Perfectly heart shaped, the amethyst seemed like a message of love when she needed it most.

Raphael on the Headstone

Love can be eternal and take different forms. One of the strongest is the passion we have for our family, and through the generations, that emotion can intensify and change.

As the family grows, the love of a grandparent also grows, due to less involvement in the day-to-day busyness of child rearing and more quality time spent with the grandkids. Someone once said a grandparent and a grandchild understand each other because they share a common foe, but it is more than that. A small sign can travel the distance of years and life experience to tell one generation that another generation is still thinking about it.

Stephany DeSantiago has loved four men in her life, and she has lived to see all of them leave her. When she was 17, her brother disappeared. Then her husband left her before their son was born and never kept in contact with his family.

But Stephany's two greatest loves were her father and her son, and she has buried both. She has stood at their graves and left flowers and said prayers. She leaves other mementos of love, too—or at least she used to. In death, the two boys she has never stopped loving or believing in have found each other, and she believes they talk to each other on some plane she cannot reach. Their connection doesn't stop there. If you believe this story, they've exchanged a gold chain, too.

The gold chain and Saint Raphael medal were not expensive, but Stephany's father, Gus, thought they were a sign from heaven, so he bought them. He had been traveling by bus nearly every night to see his sick uncle in the hospital. He got off the bus one day and found a $20 bill in the street. As he bent down to pick it up, the wind blew it onto the window of a pawn shop. Like a sign from God, it landed right above a display case containing the medal of Saint Raphael, the patron saint of the sick.

Although Gus never admitted how much the medal had cost, he said it was more than $20, but well worth the investment. His uncle got better almost immediately, and Gus felt the saint had everything to do with it.

Gus told the story often when Stephany was a child, and she felt it was a part of the family history. "We didn't have many stories. No one in our family was famous or had done anything too crazy. Daddy had that damn story, and I used to love it. I know he probably lied about most of it, but I didn't care. The telling made it real, and I guess that was enough for me," she said.

When her son, Philip, was born in 1995, Gus' energy multiplied. After her husband left, Stephany was forced to move in with her parents, but that suited them just fine—especially Gus. He loved Philly and gushed over him, and he doted on his daughter. The little boy sat in his grandfather's lap for hours, listening to him tell stories and hum songs. "He would whisper to him in Portuguese, which I never learned. I don't know what he was telling him, but Philly knew and would smile and laugh," Stephany said. "He couldn't even talk yet, but he could hear what [my father] was saying.

An example of a Saint Raphael medal.

"You know, you remember the weirdest things about someone. [Daddy] had these huge hands. I remember his smile, the chain, and his huge hands. When he picked Philly up, my little guy would disappear in Daddy's hands. He would scoop him up and there would just be his spiky hair poking out from the top of his fingers."

Gus died of pneumonia in 1997. The death came fast, and no one quite knew how to deal with it. But Stephany knew Gus must be buried with his Saint Raphael medal. She was almost beside herself with frustration when the funeral director returned it to her after Gus was buried.

"There is a policy that they can't have jewelry on so people aren't going to rob the graves. I just wanted him to have it, and they handed it back. I felt he couldn't find peace without it."

On Gus' birthday, about seven months after his death, Stephany went to the gravesite to place flowers near the headstone. As Philly slept in the carriage next to her, she dug a small hole and put the metal in the ground. She cried and laughed at the same time. "It was something he would have done," she admitted.

A week later, while finishing up homework for her nursing class, Stephany noticed something on the kitchen counter.

"It was Raphael," she said. "I had just cleaned the kitchen before getting to work, so I know it wasn't there. I saw it shine in the light and picked it up. I saw that medal my whole life and I know it like I know my own face. I can't explain it, but it was in my hand."

Being a spiritual person, Stephany viewed it as a sign: Her father was okay and didn't need it any more. "He wasn't going to be sick anymore, so maybe someone else needed it. That's the only thing I could think of," she said.

She knew the medal was for her son. She placed it on his bureau that night and kissed his forehead.

"That kid could sleep. Even as a baby he slept through the night. So I hear him up having a major conversation with someone, and I come in. It was a little after midnight, but he was sitting up in bed. He was holding the chain out in front of him and giggling. I asked him where he had gotten it, and he said Grandy gave it to him. Grandy was his name for Daddy. I asked him where Grandy was, and he pointed to the wall and said he was with Raphael. He couldn't say the name right, so it sounded more like Ralphy L."

Although she was disturbed by the incident, she also felt a bit of relief. Giving the medal to Philly had been the right decision. More importantly, her father was looking after her son. If she believed the dead could help the living—and she did—there was no reason to be scared.

She placed a stool in her son's room the next day so he could reach the medal on the bureau whenever he wanted it. Unfortunately, the idol never worked for him. Less than six months later, Stephany was in a car accident and Philly died. To this day, she refuses to share the details of what happened, but she is able to speak of what she felt afterward.

"I hurt so much I didn't want to breathe. I'm a good person with a deep faith. My brother went away, and my daddy and baby died. I didn't think I could take it," she said.

So she decided to give the medal to her son one last time. She took it straight to her son's grave a week after he was buried. She dug a small hole, buried the medal, and covered it with a rose.

"It was his. I had no one left to give it to. It got me through those weeks. I was almost obsessed with burying it. Part of me thought it would come back," Stephany said.

When she went to the cemetery to lay flowers on her father's grave, the medal was hanging on the headstone.

"I lost it. I wept so hard I almost threw up. It wasn't sadness. I knew at that moment they were together."

If she was looking for a signal from the Other Side, the medal was a mixed message. She felt in her heart it was a sign, but she didn't know what to do with it. Was it now hers to take? She thought so and carried it in her hand the whole way home. When she got back to her apartment, she placed it in an old cigar box, something she felt her father would have liked, and tucked it under her bed.

"I would still cry," Stephany said. "Sometimes I would open the box and hold [the medal] and think of them both. It was very comforting, but one of them, probably Daddy, thought it was too much. He wanted me to move on. I think he took it back."

On one particularly bad night, she reached under the bed to get the medal, and it was gone. "It was like slapping me across the face. I got it. Daddy forced me to take the training wheels off. He made me practice math. I know his way. This was him."

It was not like she never saw it again. Sometimes she sees the chain on their headstones when she visits the cemetery.

"It's not every time, and I can never tell whether it will be on Philly's or Daddy's [stone]. It is shining in the sunlight. I never touch it. I leave it there and know it will show up again sometime. I think of it as their little game with me and something they share."

Stephany has no idea where the chain goes when she isn't there. Some things can't be explained by science. She just leans on faith and believes in love.

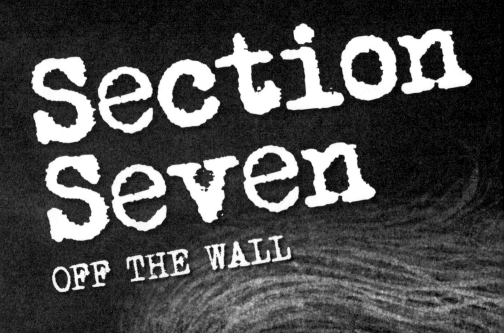

Section Seven

OFF THE WALL

Mirror, Mirror on the Wall

P eople have been gazing at their own reflections since the beginning of mankind. Imagine what it was like being the first person to bend over to get a drink from a pool of water, and to see that strange creature staring back! Over the millennia, we've perfected the art of staring at ourselves.

The first manufactured mirrors came around 6000 B.C. and were made from polished obsidian, which came from volcanic lava. The silver-backed mirror—the precursor of the aluminum-backed version we use today—was perfected in 1835 by Justus von Liebig, a German chemist who devised the process of silvering that greatly improved the use of mirrors.

And as long as mirrors have been around, they've been the subject of great superstition. Mirrors have long been said to be a reflection of the soul because they can only reflect and cannot lie. They don't reflect the person's perception (although how the person views the reflection is, of course, subjective), but rather just what is truly there, imperfections and all. That's why vampires and witches can't see their reflections in a mirror—it's believed they no longer have a soul. The vampire lost his, and the witch gave hers up willingly to the devil. That's also why hanging a mirror near your front door eventually became commonplace—not only did it allow you to see what you looked like as you were heading out the door, it also allowed you to see if those entering your house had a soul. Imagine how awkward it was if they didn't!

One of the most common superstitions regarding mirrors is that breaking one will lead to seven years' worth of bad luck. This belief likely originated with the Romans, who believed the soul renewed itself every seven years; breaking a mirror would cause a person to endure hardship until the soul could be cleansed.

As long as mirrors have been around, they've been the subject of great superstition. Mirrors have long been said to be a reflection of the soul because they can only reflect and cannot lie.

In a darkened room, you stare into a mirror and call out three times for "Bloody Mary," and she'll appear with the intention of killing you.

But why was a broken mirror considered so unlucky? The Romans, among many other ancient civilizations, also bought into the "reflection of the soul" theory about mirrors. In their view, a broken mirror meant the reflection of a broken soul.

There were ways to get around the seven years of bad luck, however; the most popular way was to take all the broken pieces of the mirror and grind them into dust. Other methods involved burying the broken pieces or setting them afloat in a southward-flowing river. Did it work? Well, when dealing with superstition, it all goes back to belief; if you believe in the curse of breaking a mirror, then why not believe in the supposed reversal of the curse?

Many cultures and religions also call for the covering of all mirrors when a person has died, but for different reasons. In the Jewish faith, mirrors are covered because the mourning period is supposed to be about the person who has passed and not about the vanity of the living. In Romania, people believe mirrors must be covered because if they are not, the spirit of the deceased may enter them and become trapped in the reflective world.

Other superstitions that deal with mirrors:

- A baby should never see its own reflection until after its first birthday; some cultures believe it will stunt the growth of their souls, others think it will bring death.
- It is bad luck to hang mirrors facing one another.
- If you think a house is haunted, hang a mirror on a south-facing wall. If there are ghosts present, the mirror will fall every time you hang it.
- Never bring home a mirror from the home of a deceased love one, or they will haunt it and you.
- If you look into a mirror in a room where someone has recently died and you see their reflection instead of your own, it means you will soon die as well.
- A couple who first sees one another in a mirror's reflection will go on to have a long and happy marriage.
- Buddhists are said to believe that negative spirits can enter the door of a house if it has a triangular-shaped roof, but it can be prevented by hanging a small circular mirror in front of the door.
- Mirrors could be used for divination or scrying, two different ways of telling the future. Included with this theory was the idea that if you stared into a mirror on Halloween, you'd see your future husband.

Mirror Legends

There are also plenty of legends that have developed over the years regarding mirrors. The best-known is that of "Bloody Mary," the long-summoned character of folklore whose origin is hard to pinpoint. The basic outline is always the same, no matter where the story is being told—in a darkened room, you stare into a mirror and call out three times for "Bloody Mary," and she'll appear with the intention of killing you. Whether the story also involves candles, spinning around three times, or any other variation, it still all comes back to the dark room, the mirror, and the chant.

The legend comes from England, and one school of thought is that it relates to Queen Mary I, who was called "Bloody Mary" for her treatment of Protestants while restoring the Roman Catholic Church to England. Others say the nickname was also used to mock her for the many miscarriages she suffered in trying to conceive an heir, even undergoing a "phantom pregnancy" in 1555 because she so badly wanted to have a child.

Some point not to Queen Mary but to a character of folklore named Mary Worth, who either murdered her own child or watched the child's murder happen, depending on the source. Her spirit is said to roam the earth, seeking to exact revenge for her child's death. To summon her, recite, "Mary Worth, I killed your baby."

Popular culture has long played a part in keeping the "Bloody Mary" myth alive, even causing it to morph over the years into two other similar legends. One is related to the Bell Witch of Adams, Tennessee, who supposedly haunted the Bell family in the early part of the 19th century. This case was loosely adapted into the movie, *An American Haunting*, and is the only example in the history of the U.S. Justice System where a spirit was blamed for a murder in a court of law. Local legend in Tennessee states that even today, if you say, "I don't believe in the Bell Witch" over and over again in a mirror, she will appear and scare you until you do believe.

Another more recent example is that of the Candyman. Originally created by horror writer Clive Barker in his short story, "The Forbidden," the character was adapted for a 1992 horror film, *Candyman*. The Candyman, the son of a slave,

In addition to offering a reflection of us and maybe the reflection of our souls, some mirrors also contain a reflection of the past.

Saying "Candyman" five times, while looking into a mirror, will summon him. At left is how he appears in the movie, *Candyman*.

was a well-known artist who impregnated a white woman.

He was punished by having his drawing hand cut off (replaced by a hook), covered in honey, and then stung to death by bees. Intent on killing anyone who calls him by the taunting nickname of "Candyman," he can be summoned by calling his name five times while staring in a mirror, similar to Bloody Mary. In the film—the first of a trilogy—his curse is prevalent throughout a poverty-stricken, gang-ridden neighborhood in Chicago.

Even though this character is fictional, it hasn't stopped the Candyman legend from capturing the imaginations of those who have been born since the film's release. He's still just as feared and as frequently summoned as Bloody Mary among today's youth, especially in urban neighborhoods.

But is there more to mirrors than the eye can see? In addition to offering a reflection of us and maybe the reflection of our souls, some mirrors also contain a reflection of the past. It's embedded in the aluminum and the glass and frequently rises to the surface.

Take, for example, the mirror that hangs in a hallway of The Myrtles Plantation in St. Francisville, Louisiana. Considered by many to be among the most haunted places in America, the plantation is now a bed and breakfast whose alleged hauntings have been featured on television programs such as *Unsolved Mysteries* and *Ghost Hunters*.

Originally built by former Pennsylvania lawyer David Bradford in 1796, the plantation was eventually passed on to his daughter, Sara, and her husband, local judge Clark Woodruff, in the 1820s. The Woodruffs lived on the plantation with their three children—Cornelia, James, and Mary. According to the legends, the Woodruffs also had slaves, one of whom was a beautiful young girl named Chloe. She was glad when she was asked to give up the hard labor of working in the fields in order to serve as governess to the Woodruff children, so much so that she easily gave in to the sexual advances of Judge

Woodruff, a notorious womanizer. For a while, Chloe thought she was safe—as long as she was sleeping with Woodruff, she would remain in the house.

However, he soon began to grow tired of her as his mistress, and Chloe feared that meant she would soon be turned back out into the fields. Paranoid, she would often eavesdrop on conversations Woodruff had behind closed doors, listening in through the keyhole. When he caught her, Judge Woodruff cut off one of her ears as punishment. For the rest of her short life, Chloe kept her head wrapped in a green turban so no one would see the missing ear. An earring was pinned where the ear would have been.

Chloe didn't seek her revenge right away; instead, she continued to serve in the house, yet her paranoia about being sent back into the fields never abated. She hatched a plan in which she would give the family a small amount of poison to make them ill, and then prove her worth by nursing them back to health. She put her plan into motion by adding crushed oleander leaves to a cake she was baking for Cornelia's upcoming birthday. However, Chloe put in far too much oleander, and Sara, Cornelia, and James all died as a result. Judge Woodruff and Baby Mary, who had not eaten the cake, survived.

When Chloe told another slave how the Woodruffs had died—admitting that she was the cause—the slaves were fearful that Judge Woodruff would punish them all for the crime. To curry favor, they lynched Chloe and hung her from a tree. Once they were sure she was dead, her body was weighted with rocks and thrown into a nearby river.

In the ensuing years, a ghostly figure was seen roaming the grounds of The Myrtles—easily identifiable by her green turban and single earring. Chloe's spirit still wanders the grounds today, and many feel that she can be seen in the hallway mirror that allegedly once hung in the dining room where she served the poisoned cake.

Chloe's ghost isn't the only one seen in the mirror; visitors often report seeing Sara Woodruff and her children in it as well. The legend is that Judge Woodruff sealed off the dining room after the death of his wife and children and never allowed it to be opened again during his time there. As a result, that mirror was left uncovered during Chloe's lynching and during the mourning period for his family; hence, their spirits were all trapped inside its reflection.

These days, as it hangs in the hallway, the mirror is also subject to mysterious smudges that cannot be wiped away, despite being cleaned repeatedly and the glass being replaced on more than one occasion.

There are some problems with the legend of Chloe, however; for one, there's no record that there ever was a slave by that name serving at The

> The faces seen in the mirror could just
> be the result of pareidolia ... like seeing
> Jesus in your grilled cheese sandwich or
> the face of a man in the moon.

Myrtles. That's easy enough to explain because slave records weren't always precise in those days. In addition, the actual cause of death listed for Sara and her children is yellow fever. Was this just a cover-up for a heinous act committed by a scorned slave woman? Or is the legend just a better story than the truth?

The faces seen in the mirror could just be the result of pareidolia (sometimes called "matrixing") in which our brain looks for familiar patterns in the random chaos of visual or auditory evidence. It's like seeing Jesus in your grilled cheese sandwich or the face of a man in the moon. Those streaks in the mirror are simply perceived as being faces, because that's what they most resemble.

There are some reports that the mirror itself was not even in the house during the time of the murders; instead, it was purchased by James and Frances Myers, who owned the plantation in the 1970s and were the ones who first began to bring attention to the hauntings there. It is said that Frances Myers actually purchased the mirror from an antiques dealer in the French Quarter of New Orleans, despite reports that it was haunted. She felt it would fit right in with both the décor and the ghosts that already roamed The Myrtles.

Marilyn in the Mirror

While Chloe may have become famous for her image in the mirror at The Myrtles, at the Hollywood Roosevelt Hotel there's a mirror that still reflects the image of one of the most famous women who ever lived.

The Hollywood Roosevelt opened in 1927, financed by some of Tinseltown's elite, such as Douglas Fairbanks, Mary Pickford, and Louis B. Mayer. It was intended to be the destination point for the stars, and it has lived up to that reputation over the years. In fact, many famous ghosts still roam its halls today. One of the most seen is the spirit of actor Montgomery Clift, who stayed in the hotel while filming the 1953 classic, *From Here to Eternity.*

But the most sought-after spirit is that of blonde bombshell Marilyn Monroe, who called the Roosevelt home on more than one occasion. Marilyn lived there when she first started to hit it big as a model, and she fell in love with the hotel. She especially loved Suite 1200 and the large mirror that hung on its wall.

Sometime after Marilyn's death in 1962, the mirror was moved out of Suite 1200.

Before haunting the mirror at the Roosevelt Hotel, Marilyn Monroe studies her lines in this 1955 photo taken in the studio of photographer Milton Greene.

The rumor is that it was placed in the manager's office and that a housekeeper was cleaning it one day when Marilyn's image appeared in the mirror. By this time, the hotel was already becoming famous for its many Hollywood ghosts, so it seemed only natural to put the Marilyn mirror on display. It was placed in the lobby near the elevators, and visitors by the scores still report seeing the iconic beauty's image reflected back at them. Of course, that could have something to do with the fact that the hotel placed an engraving of Marilyn on the wall right next to it—even though it's merely a portrait of her face. The ghostly sightings include Marilyn in all her full-figured glory and in a variety of fashions, as if she stepped out of *Gentlemen Prefer Blondes* and into the mirror itself.

As Marilyn once sang, diamonds may be a girl's best friend, but a mirror is apparently the best way of keeping one foot in this world while advancing to the Great Beyond.

Sacrifice

A spirit does not always make itself known with a loud shout. Sometimes the impact of the paranormal can be subtle, almost unnoticeable, until you happen upon it, and a normal part of your day is suddenly no longer normal.

Whether the communication is a bang or a whimper, the emotional punch may be just as moving, especially when the message being sent is one of love.

Josie believes she is either blessed or cursed with an ability to connect to those who have died. She has always felt attracted to the other side, and often gets odd feelings and sees things in places where other people have reported ghosts. Almost every house she has lived in since she was a child has experienced some kind of spectral commotion. She currently resides in an area that seems to have heightened paranormal activity. Known as the Glen, neighbors tell tales of the spirits they see and the unexplained things they experience.

Her most uplifting experience involves her husband from her first marriage. Unlike her other stories, she was on the outside of this one, watching the events as they unfolded. She is the only one who understands the significance of what she saw and the true meaning of sacrifice. When she shares it, her voice has a different tone than when she tells tales of ghostly people walking through her house or dark figures in her windows. This experience has special meaning for her, and as she battles sickness in her own life, the story takes on a different significance.

Josie's first husband, Frank, was diagnosed with cancer. He kept his hopes up, but it was not the first time he had faced the disease and the outcome did not look good. As the months went on, the tumors continued to grow, and while Josie, who has always been drawn to the medical field and currently works as a nurse, tried to console him, they both knew what the future held. The doctors gave him worse news at each visit, and they both braced themselves before each appointment.

Even more disturbed by the news, however, was Frank's mother, Eileen. Frank was her only son and her emotional grounding, but she was close to giving up on herself and on him. She was an alcoholic and suffered from asthma. As Frank got sicker, Eileen sank deeper into depression and turned to her faith. She began to beg God to save her son.

"She would sit there and drink and cry all the time. 'Just take me. Let him live.' It was a real thing for her. I don't think she could imagine burying her son," Josie said.

Then Eileen developed cancer herself. The doctors told her it was not as dangerous as Frank's, but she needed to have a hysterectomy. It was autumn before she had the surgery because the doctors had issued requirements involving her alcoholism that needed to be met before the surgery could be performed.

"There were a few months between her diagnosis and the surgery, so she was sick for a while. I heard her say something about it being the bargain she made, but Frank didn't get better. He was getting sicker and so was she. Actually she was pretty loud about it. She kept asking why God wasn't living up to his end. Why would he curse them both?" Josie said.

Josie remembers the day of Eileen's surgery perfectly, even nearly two decades later. It was a bitter autumn day in New England. As she opened the door to her house, leaves began to swirl around her, although she hadn't noticed any wind as she walked from her car to the house. The sounds of the outside world faded away and she got an eerie feeling. Like a movie on pause, time stopped. Then the phone rang inside the house. "And I just knew it," Josie said. Eileen had died of an asthma attack in the recovery room.

Josie does not like to speak ill of the dead, but she said Eileen was never a friendly or warm woman. Most people who knew her thought she was a sad person, even before the drinking became an all-consuming part of her life. Josie thinks about this when she tells what happens next, unsure if the sign her mother-in-law left behind was to bring peace to people or to let everyone know what she gave up for her son.

That day, Josie and Frank went to her house. Josie was the first to notice the picture of Eileen and her husband from their 25th wedding anniversary, where a halo had formed around Eileen's face. She thought it was just coincidence, laughed to herself, and tried to forget about it.

As the funeral approached, the picture grew darker. Josie kept returning to the picture to see if it had changed. Each time she did, it was darker.

"I pointed it out to Frank and he started to cry. He said it wasn't there before, and the picture was not that old. I told him it had changed, and he just slowly nodded his head at me. I don't think he really wanted to accept it."

In the weeks following the funeral, they washed the frame and cleaned the picture, but it continued to get darker until it became a bright orange-yellow. At the same time, Frank went into remission without chemo or any further treatment.

Since 1982, Frank has lived cancer-free and with no serious health problems. He keeps the picture of his mother displayed as a sign of what she sacrificed for him.

Josie herself is now battling cancer, made even more dangerous by other health complications she has lived with for years. She is not sure if there is someone like Eileen in her life who would trade places with her when her time comes, but she finds comfort knowing her mother-in-law was able to make contact.

"There is definitely something out there after we die. Whenever I get sad or scared, I think about that picture. It used to scare me, but now it makes me feel hope."

Masking Evil

"Evil comes to all us men of imagination, wearing as its mask all the virtues."
—*Irish poet and dramatist William Butler Yeats*

For as long as man has been conscious of his own image, he's also felt the need to conceal it. Whether for purposes of entertainment, concealment, or reverence, masks have been used whenever there was a need to express something that the actual visage could not. As an expression frozen in time, a mask provides power and force that no mere face can equal. Sometimes that force is evil, and can remain attached to the mask long after whatever dark ceremony forged it has subsided from memory.

In November 2007, Jeannette, a longtime paranormal investigator and demonologist, and her family moved into their dream home in an upscale country club gated community in Palm Springs, California. They moved there to be closer to Jeannette's brother, who had been diagnosed with liver cancer. Even though the circumstances for the move were less than ideal, the house was perfect.

For a little while, anyway.

As a housewarming gift to herself, Jeannette purchased two Haitian masks from Port-au-Prince, Haiti. They were large and heavy, beautifully carved of solid mahogany, and Jeannette adored them. She had long been a collector of masks from around the world, and now that she had her perfect home, these masks would be the centerpiece of it and of her collection.

The room where the masks took center stage.

But right from the beginning, something wasn't right about these masks—even before they'd been removed from their original shipping crates. Jeannette's husband, Bob, packed his truck with boxes to move to the new place, including the box containing the masks. While driving on the freeway, the truck began to accelerate on its own. No matter what he tried, Bob couldn't slow it down; it was as if the brakes were disconnected and the truck just kept going faster and faster, even shifting into neutral. With some

The masks that caused much turmoil for the family.

quick thinking, Bob drove up a steep exit ramp and jammed the emergency brake as hard as he could, stopping the truck.

"He was quite shaken up by the incident," Jeannette said. "He had the truck checked out a few days later, and the mechanic found no problems with it."

Once the masks were unpacked in the new house, Jeannette gave them a wall of their own. She hung them in the dining room, the biggest and most central room of the house. That didn't sit well with her then 12-year-old son, who never liked the masks and didn't want to see them hanging on any wall, let alone one he'd have to look at every day.

The family's dog was well trained and behaved, yet once the masks were hung on the wall, she refused to cross the dining room. It was a strange behavior she had never exhibited before, and hasn't since. The family had to carry or push her across the floor just to get her from one side of the room to the other.

"I'm still not sure if she was afraid of those masks, or if she could just sense or hear what we couldn't," Jeannette said.

It wasn't long before strange phenomena started occurring. At first, Jeannette didn't think anything of it—paranormal activity always seemed to find her family, no matter where they lived. But soon, the weird things taking place went beyond just regular ghostly goings-on.

One day Bob was at work and Jeannette and her son were in the backyard playing on their trampoline. When they came back into the house, they found broken glass strewn across the floor, making a nearly 70-foot path from the back door to the kitchen counter, where a heavy drinking glass had originally been placed. Though not easily breakable, the heavy glass had shattered, its path of shards trailing around two corners. Jeannette started cleaning up the

The youngest son was hit with such force that red, upside down finger marks appeared on his forehead.

mess, and when she got close to the front door, she noticed a dead bird sprawled on the floor in the entranceway—even though the entire house was locked, except for the back door, and the security system was armed. There was no way the bird could have made it into the house without anyone knowing.

A couple of months later, Jeannette's oldest son came home from his third deployment in Iraq, bringing along a large group of friends and fellow soldiers who were going to spend their 30-day leave participating in paintball tournaments in the area. They were all hanging around the dining room and kitchen area when another one of the heavy drinking glasses, sitting on the dining room table, exploded. It broke with such force that the shards covered the entire 25-foot-by-30-foot dining room floor. It freaked out everyone in the house.

"These were experienced combat soldiers, and they all slept together on the living room floor that night or huddled in pairs," Jeannette said. "And they slept with all the lights on."

More dead birds were found inside and outside the house, including one inexplicably stuffed with straw.

Shattering glass was only the beginning as the phenomena began to escalate. Soon, a loud banging started rattling the walls, first in the kitchen and then on the inside and outside of her youngest son's bedroom. The activity took a turn for the worse when the youngest son was awakened by the feeling of being slapped by unseen hands at the same time the banging was taking place. One time, he was hit with such force and from such an odd angle that red, upside down finger marks appeared on his forehead.

"It looked like he had been slapped hard by someone or something very tall," Jeannette said.

When the family realized the bangs were occurring with some regularity, Jeannette decided to time them. For months, they happened every day at 10:19 a.m. One morning, Jeannette decided to leave a digital audio recorder running on the kitchen counter while she went to get her son from school. Nobody was in the house, but when she played the recording back, she was shocked to not only hear the loud banging, but also unintelligible screams as well. Jeannette sent the audio clips to others in the paranormal field, and all agreed it was unlike anything they'd ever heard.

Not long after, Bob took a job out of state, leaving Jeannette and her youngest son alone in the house. Even with all the weird commotions going on, she wanted to stay there to remain close to her dying brother.

After visiting her brother one evening, Jeannette and her son came home to find the dining room door open and the dog—who always greeted them at the door—missing. Food from the cupboards and refrigerator was strewn all about the floor, creating a path that led to the two Haitian masks. The house was large and they were afraid to look for an intruder on their own, so Jeannette called 911 while her son closed the back door. The police arrived and searched the house and garage thoroughly. Everything was secured from the inside and showed no signs of entry or any type of disturbance. Nothing was missing. The police theorized that the intruder had entered the house, was scared by the dog, and then ran out the back door with the dog chasing behind him.

As they stood in the kitchen discussing the break-in, they heard a noise in the garage. They found the dog there—though she had not been in the garage earlier when the police checked it, and the doors were still secured from the inside. It was as if the dog had disappeared and then reappeared from thin air.

"The police had no explanation for where the dog had come from, and neither did we. We still don't know to this day," Jeanette said. "But after that, we'd always hear voices and boxes moving in the garage, yet every time, it was empty and secured from the inside."

The phenomena kept intensifying—the banging, the slapping of her son, the breaking glass. More dead birds were found inside and outside the house, including one inexplicably stuffed with straw. It finally reached the point where Jeanette had to call a good friend, paranormal investigator John Zaffis. John, who began his career investigating claims of the unexplained and the demonic alongside his legendary aunt and uncle, investigators and demonologists Ed and Lorraine Warren, is widely considered the world's foremost authority on haunted, possessed, and cursed objects. He even operates his own paranormal museum at his Connecticut home, John Zaffis Museum of the Paranormal, with thousands of such items on display.

Zaffis felt that because of the age of Jeannette's son and the family's history with the paranormal, they might be the victim of a poltergeist. Poltergeist means "noisy ghost" in German, but in actuality, the prevailing theory is that they're not the actual ghosts of deceased persons. Instead, they're either a mischievous spirit energy that exists solely to plague people or—a newer theory—are actually caused through unconscious mental abilities manifesting in a prepubescent child. When Jeannette mentioned the correlation between the activity and the arrival of the Haitian masks, Zaffis suggested she cover them for a while to see if anything changed.

"In hindsight, I should have taken them down, but I just covered them with an Army Ranger flag instead," Jeannette said.

Once the masks were covered, the activity did subside. When a friend of her youngest son died in a freak accident not long after, the family decided it would be best if her son went to stay with his older brother in Kansas for a while. That left Jeannette home alone in the house, along with the family dog and a new puppy they brought home to help ease the young boy's pain over the death of his friend.

"Once my son was safely out of the house, it didn't take long before the investigator in me came out," Jeannette said. "I invited another investigator from the East Coast to spend the summer in my home to help me document the activity."

It only took three nights before that investigator became just as terrified as Jeannette's family.

On that third night, the investigator felt something kicking the bed and awoke to see a shadow person standing there, blocking the light. The next morning the investigator told Jeannette it was "the most frightening experience" of their life. After that, the two slept on opposite sides of the house. The activity continued, along with the addition of music and voices in the dining room at night. The sounds would stop whenever someone entered the room, but then start again once the dining room was empty.

In late August, Jeannette's brother passed away and the other investigator returned home. Jeannette spent the rest of the summer alone in the house. Within a month, the electricity on the side of the house where the masks hung went out completely. Not long after, the plumbing on that side of the house stopped working as well. In the dining room itself, the light on the ceiling fan flickered day and night.

"It got to the point where I didn't enter that side of the house," Jeannette said. "Yet I didn't want to take the masks down, either. It was almost as if I was drawn to them, as much as they disturbed me."

Two days before Halloween, a family member came to visit and asked why there was a big hole by the front door, inside the gate. Jeannette never used the front door, as she came and went through the garage. She was blown away to find a 6-foot-by-8-foot hole right next to the front door. It was five feet deep, and Jeannette could see the pipes leading into her house. She called the gas company to check for leaks. When the gas man jumped into the hole to check, the ground underneath him gave way. The hole was now about 15 feet deep, with water rushing in two directions. The two quick-fixed the hole by placing plywood over it and securing the perimeter with police tape as a warning. That same week, Jeannette noticed another sink hole in her front yard, this one 20 feet in diameter. It was as if the house itself was being dragged into the depths of hell.

Inside the house, Jeannette began hearing "tinking" noises from the eight-foot arched windows in the dining room, as if they were bending and stressed. She also started to hear deep pops coming from the dining room floor.

"I was very afraid because I know the deeper the sound, the bigger the hole," she said. "I began having nightmares about giant sinkholes under my home and water running through Swiss cheese-like tunnels."

Jeannette asked a friend who was a contractor to examine the sink holes and tell her the extent of the damage. He said it was bad. He told her to get everything out of the house

It was as if the house itself was being dragged into the depths of hell.

before calling the city, or else the city would "red tag" the house and she wouldn't be allowed back in, it was that unsafe.

While all this was going on, Jeannette became depressed. She asked Bob to come home and help move them out of the house, so he drove from Idaho in a new $40,000 company truck. The day after he arrived, the truck was stolen from the driveway of the house, only to be found abandoned a mile down the road.

Bob decided to quit his out-of-state job and stay home with his wife. Soon he, too, fell into a deep depression, remaining in a dark room in the house for an entire week, something out of character for him. He, too, avoided the side of the house with the masks, and he refused to acknowledge the sounds that were coming from the dining room.

Eventually, Bob shook himself out of his funk and got a new job in Arizona. He found a new place for the family to live and rented a big truck to move their belongings from California. Jeannette took an extra day to say goodbye to her family, and with the masks in a box in her car, headed to the new house. But before leaving, she contacted Zaffis—there was no way she was going to bring those masks into her new home. She didn't even want to risk driving across the desert with them in her car. She figured the best place for them was in Zaffis' museum.

With the last of their belongings, Jeannette drove to a family member's house three miles away to leave the masks. When she got to the second stop sign of her trip, the box with the masks flew forward with such force it pushed the driver's seat forward, pinning Jeannette against the steering wheel. She was nearly broadsided by another car, and had to wiggle out the passenger side door to get out of the car, hurting her knee on the steering column in the process. She threw the box containing the masks into the trunk of the car. When she arrived at her relative's house, she left the box outside because nobody wanted it inside. Then Jeannette drove to Arizona where she and her family have lived in peace without any further disturbances.

Meanwhile, the masks never did make it to John Zaffis in Connecticut. The next day, when Jeannette's relative went to take the box to the post office, it was gone.

"I guess they are someone else's problem now, and I hope they fare better with them than we did," Jeannette said. "They ruined our dream home and nearly tore our family apart. They frightened seasoned investigators and baffled policemen. They put us in danger, and I am glad they're gone. And now I am far more careful about what I allow to come into my home."

The Haunted Painting

In February 2000, a painting appeared on the auction website eBay under the heading "Haunted Painting." In truth, it was a painting titled *The Hands Resist Him* by artist Bill Stoneham. But the truth should never stand in the way of a good ghost story.

Stoneham painted the picture in 1972 and it depicts a young boy standing on a doorstep next to a creepy life-sized girl doll. Behind him, in the glass panes of the door, numerous sets of hands reach for him and press up against the glass. Stoneham has stated on his website that the boy is his younger self and the hands represent other lives. The doll serves as his guide between the waking world and the dreaming world, as represented by the door.

The painting was first purchased in the early 1970s by John Marley, a noted character actor who had roles in films including *The Godfather*. According to Stoneham, the owner of the gallery where the painting was shown and the *Los Angeles Times* art critic who reviewed the show were both dead within a year after gazing upon the painting.

Marley owned the painting until his own death in 1984, and at some point it ended up on the grounds of an old brewery, where a California couple found it and took it home. Their four-and-a-half-year-old daughter complained that at night she could hear the figures in the painting arguing, and that the doll would force the boy to exit the painting and enter the room in which it was hanging. In order to prove nothing was happening, the father set up some motion-activated cameras in front of the painting. The family was shocked when, on the third night, they captured what looked like the boy coming out of the painting. The object in the doll's hands (which according to Stoneham was just a dry-cell battery and some wires) had morphed into a gun, which the doll had pointed at the boy as if to force him out of the painting.

The couple listed the artwork as "Haunted Painting" on eBay, and included the photos of the boy allegedly leaving the painting. The eBay listing had the following warning posted as well: "Do not bid on this painting if you are susceptible to stress-related disease, faint of heart or are unfamiliar with supernatural events ... This painting may or may not possess supernatural powers that could impact or change your life ... "

The auction description went on in rambling fashion, at first attempting to offer photographic proof that the figures could exit the painting before later claiming, "There are no ghosts in this world, no supernatural powers, this is just a painting" and that it is "pure entertainment."

Once the item was on eBay, the alleged hauntings took on a whole new dimension.

Over 13,000 people viewed the auction, and many reported having paranormal experiences of their own. Just the image on the website alone was enough to impact those who viewed it, from feelings of queasiness to intense heat radiating from the computer monitor. The couple selling the painting put an addendum on the auction listing suggesting that people "not use this image as the background on the screen" and "not display this image around juveniles or children."

The 30-day auction, which began at $199, received 30 bids, and the painting finally sold for $1,025. Although the buyer remained anonymous, there have been numerous websites tracking the tale that suggest nothing paranormal happened to the new owners.

The Other Haunted Painting

In 1985, a series of mysterious fires broke out across England, with one common thread running through them—in each home, everything burned to the ground, except for a print of a painting known as *The Crying Boy*. The painting, by artist Bruno Amadio, depicts a close-up of a young boy with tears streaming down his cheeks. Around 50,000 prints of the painting were sold across England, and there are also some variations painted by Amadio that appear to be part of the curse as well.

The story first came to light when a fireman spoke to a British newspaper, which printed reports of dozens of other fires that had occurred, with a print of the painting remaining untouched. The paper called for other prints to be mailed to its newsroom to be set ablaze in a big bonfire to quell whatever curse was attached.

Yet the mysterious fires still continued, and the legend of *The Crying Boy* grew. According to the story, Amadio had taken in a young orphan—the subject of the painting—whose parents had died in a fire just as strange as the ones later associated with the painting, and that it was the boy who set their home ablaze. He was a proven firebug, and some even suggested he was actually a pyrokinetic—someone who can start fires with their mind. Amadio failed to heed the warnings, however, and not long after the boy arrived, the artist's studio burned to the ground.

Ten years later, the boy died in a fiery car crash, and from that day forward, any paintings of him carried his curse and ignited into flames.

In later years, the newspaper tried to prove the reason the prints didn't burn in the fires was due to the string that was used on the back of them: once the string ignited, the print would fall to the floor and remain unharmed. That may explain how the paintings survived the fires, but it cannot explain how the fires started.

Perhaps whatever caused that orphan boy so much pain and suffering still burns inside his restless spirit today.

One of the
variations of "The
Crying Boy."

Poster Child

Posters are snapshots of the trends that mark our lives. They are time capsules we tear down as we find new interests and replace with new definitions of ourselves. They are literally pictures into our hearts and desires. The best ones are framed behind glass, but most are stuck to walls with push pins and globs of putty.

Posters can also be a focus for energy left behind, a way for specters to communicate with us. While few people admit a poster is powerful enough to call them back from the dead, stories do exist about ghosts offering their opinion on the way we decorate.

Dodie, from the story on P. 24, whose house featured more than one spirit and who had her hands full with some haunted dresses, also dealt with an offended art critic. Her teenage son had placed a revealing poster of some women on his wall. The spirits, perhaps those of the little girls who had died in the house, didn't care for his choice of artwork.

"He woke up and [the poster] was thrown against the opposite wall," Dodie said. "The tack that kept it up was still in the wall. It's impossible that it just fell. He put up a nice one of some cars (instead)."

Paranormal investigator and author Thomas D'Agostino had his own poster experience when he and his wife, Arlene, moved into new living quarters. In a house where the walls are covered with swords, old instruments, gargoyles, and other eclectic artifacts, the poster should have fit right in.

"My sister bought us an original poster from the movie, *Night of the Living Dead*, from 1968," D'Agostino said. "It was quite a macabre and grotesque piece of art, fashioned in black and white. The poster definitely put across the frightening aspect of the movie.

"We decided to hang it at the top of the stairs in the old house we were renting. The house was already haunted, but the spirits liked what we had done to the rooms and we had no problem until that night."

It seemed the spirits did not like the D'Agostinos' poster. "All during the night, we heard restless shuffling and banging around upstairs. I finally went to the stairs to see what the din was, and the upstairs had a yellow hue to it. The poster, at the top of the stairs, was within the distinct discolored air. Arlene and I would hear the noises all night, and upon examining the second story, found it heavy with energy and the strange hue in the air."

While not scared, they decided the poster had to go. There was no reason to upset the balance they had struck with their unseen housemates. "In the morning, we took the poster down. At that point, the hue cleared up and a peaceful silence came over the upstairs once again. We can only deduce that the other inhabitants of the house did not like that poster at all and were very animated in letting us know."

There is one story about a haunted poster that is so disturbing, I hesitate to even tell it. It feels like someone else's secret, and in many ways it is. It involves one of the most infamous suicides in modern-day American history, a moment that defined the angst of Generation X and was blamed for the teenage violence that would follow it.

This story was shared with me years ago, and while I remember the details clearly, I can't confirm any of them. Looking back on it now, the story has too many holes, yet at the same

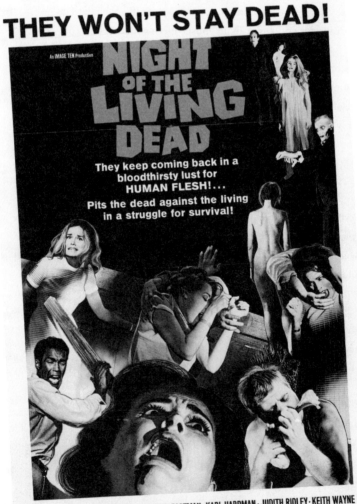

A 1968 *Night of the Living Dead* poster similar to the one at the center of a paranormal stir in the D'Agostino household.

time, is entirely too neat. I will share the story as it was told to me by a friend, who heard it from someone who was friends with the teen who experienced it. It will sound like an urban legend, but there are already so many legends surrounding this incident that I feel one more can't hurt.

On Jan. 8, 1991, Jeremy Wade Delle stepped into his English class and committed suicide while his classmates watched. The event took place before the rise of gun violence in schools that has marked our culture since, and the students at Richardson High School in Richardson, Texas, saw their lives changed forever. There has been much written about the details of that day, especially after the band Pearl Jam made the story famous with their hit song, "Jeremy," and its graphic video.

Though the room where the tragedy occurred was reopened as a classroom, it eventually was turned into a storage area for old desks. Several students reported that some time after the shooting, after school hours, a gunshot could be heard coming from the room, and at times desks stored there would be overturned or thrown against the wall.

The story I heard, which involved Jeremy's best friend at the time, was told to me by a friend of that teen's girlfriend. The news has always painted Jeremy as a sad child, and while the press and the band have stressed this, he did have a few close friends.

Jeremy and his closest friend had made a suicide pact, and while Jeremy lived up to his end of the bargain, the other teen did not. This friend was consumed by guilt and rumored to be under the influence of drugs. He kept hearing Jeremy's voice asking him why he had not killed himself yet. He even once saw the outline of his friend against a steamy bathroom mirror.

One night it all came to a head. He laid in bed, staring at a poster he and Jeremy had hung on the ceiling. The poster featured a popular band they both liked. Before Jeremy's suicide, the two would often gaze at it and talk about music and life.

As the boy thought about Jeremy that night, the four thumbtacks used to attach the poster to the ceiling fell on his face, even the tacks that should have naturally fallen near his feet. While he watched the poster hang in midair, his old friend's voice continued to ask him why he was still alive. After more than a minute, the poster floated down and spread out like a blanket over him.

The teen did not kill himself as Jeremy urged. At the time I heard the story, more than 15 years ago, he had turned his life around. The girl who told me the story hasn't talked to either the boy or his girlfriend since. I am not sure what happened to him after that, although it seems the final communication from his departed friend had the opposite effect than what was intended. The teen and his story—much like Jeremy, whose pain became a hit song—is now part of the landscape of rumor.

WRAPPING YOUR HEAD
- AND YOUR HANDS -
AROUND HAUNTED OBJECTS

Getting Attached

The blanket that Grandma made for you when you were a baby. The doll that always sat on a chair in Aunt Mary's bedroom. Grandpa's favorite pipe.

When someone dies, it's not unusual for those left behind to want a keepsake, some sort of physical object that reminds them of the deceased. It may be an item that was given to them by a loved one or that belonged to the loved one, a reminder to the living of the person who is gone. It can be as profound as wanting to move into their house or as mundane as wanting a simple tchotchke. Some of the keepsakes may seem strange to the outside observer, but they may have deep meaning to the person in mourning and help with the grieving process.

And apparently, it works from the "other side" as well.

Sometimes those who have died are not ready to give up a special object. They still want to own it, cling to it, or perhaps even use it as a conduit to stay connected with those they've left behind.

Paranormal researchers often talk about "attachment theory." This is not to be confused with the work of psychoanalyst John Bowlby, who devised his attachment theory regarding the interactions between human beings. Instead, the paranormal theory is more about entity or spirit attachment—the ability to imprint energy on people, places, or things. Whether to the living or the deceased, these objects matter. They take on a significance that goes beyond just material possession. The most inconsequential trinket can become a means to connect with the Great Beyond.

Most cases of attachment to an object turn out to be nothing more than a residual haunt; that is, it's just the leftover energy of a person that is attached, so it is unable to interact with the living. But there are plenty of instances in which it is an intelligent haunt, and therefore, communication or interaction with the spirit is possible.

The concept of spirit attachment leads to a debate among paranormal researchers when it comes to the idea of a haunted location: We look for factors in the location that can explain why it is haunted, such as a quartz rock in the foundation to retain energy or nearby running water to charge the ions in the air and amplify the energy. But isn't it possible that the spirit has just chosen to attach itself to the spot? Isn't a building nothing more than a large object?

Attachment isn't limited to just objects, either; it's just as likely for a spirit to attach itself to a person. This can happen either intentionally or by accident—many paranormal

Some people believe spirits can move between our dimension and theirs, bringing and taking objects with them.

investigators have reported "bringing home" spirits who've become attached to them during an investigation. Some will even say a protection prayer or conduct a ceremony before investigating, in order to keep any spirits from attaching to them purposely or inadvertently.

Even if an object doesn't attach itself to a person or an object, it can still focus on one. A reported sign of spirit activity is a phenomenon known as apportation, in which objects mysteriously appear or disappear through the influence of spirits. Ever wondered why your car keys are never where you left them, or why that one sock keeps disappearing in the dryer? The answer might not be as simple as you think. Spirits that can manipulate objects may be moving them in order to capture attention or announce their presence, putting them somewhere other than where they were last seen. One theory suggests that spirits can actually bring solid materials into their own dimension, thus causing them to outright disappear, before bringing them back into this plane.

Another side of apportation involves the spirit bringing an object through to our world that might not have been here previously. One example in this book, on P. 142, involves the St. Christopher's medal that appeared out of nowhere to help a family through some trying times. It was not their medal and never had been, yet it showed up when they most needed it. Did the spirit bring it into creation, or was it apported from some other location? The jury is still out on that, but the stories in which the phenomenon occurs continue.

There's one more concept of how material objects relate to paranormal activity, called a trigger object. Trigger objects are designed to get a "rise" out of a spirit, through some sort of connection the spirit has with it or a similar item. It's an experimental way to make contact; the spirit doesn't have to be actually attached to the object in order for it to work. For example, if a young woman who has died was fond of a certain doll, bringing that doll into a location she is suspected to haunt might entice her to make herself known.

Just as they can be susceptible to spirit attachments, people, too, can serve as trigger objects—especially when the spirit is considered to be dark or even evil in nature. When investigating an old prison and trying to make contact with the spirit of a serial rapist, a woman might be placed alone in his former cell in order to serve as the trigger object and draw him out.

Trigger objects don't have to be physical items, either; sometimes playing music of a certain era or speaking in a particular language or dialect can serve to activate paranormal activity.

For all the research that has been done on attachment theory in recent years, it's still unclear how or why it occurs. The best guess, however, is that most spirit attachment happens because the spirit wants it to happen. That gives a whole new meaning to the expression that one person's trash is another person's treasure.

Hands-on Experience

Psychic medium Pam Patalano has been touched with a gift, and touch is a big part of how she uses it.

"You'd be surprised what's haunted and what's not," she said. "It's all in how you handle it."

"Handle" is the operative word. Pam practices psychometry, a type of extra sensory perception in which touching and holding an object can reveal its history through psychic means.

The term psychometry was coined by Joseph Rodes Buchanan in 1842. Buchanan, a physician and professor of physiology at the Eclectic Medical Institute in Covington, Kentucky, used psychometry as a means to "measure the soul." It was embraced by the Spiritualist movement beginning in the late 1840s, and although Buchanan himself was a Spiritualist, he believed that spirits do not come into play when practicing psychometry. Instead, it centers on the psychic abilities of a person to perceive the soul; as the "psychometer," this person is responsible for measuring and interpreting whatever energies might be attached to an object.

Nearly 170 years later, Pam agrees.

"Basically, I refer to it as 'object recognition,' " she said. "Touching an object is no different than touching a person's hand. If there's an emotion attached to it, I can pick up on it."

Although the object is the focus of her attention, it's not the physical item itself that carries the spirit.

"Everything in the universe has an energy field that radiates all around it," she said. "These emotions, these impressions, they are absorbed within that energy field. It's not necessarily inside the object, but it exists in that energy field. I read that energy.

"I pick up an object, close my hands around it, and I start getting images. If there was an emotion attached to it—if somebody loved it, used it to kill somebody, whatever—I can see it. Sometimes I'll hear a message without seeing anything, but more often it's like seeing a film."

But unlike a residual haunting, in which the same scene plays over and over again, the images often change using psychometry.

"It's not the same thing all the time. I can pick up different 'movie clips'

"I pick up an object, close my hands around it, and I start getting images. If there was an emotion attached to it - if somebody loved it, used it to kill somebody, whatever - I can see it."

Yard sales can be a battleground of haunted objects.

from it, so to speak," she said. "It's not the same picture over and over again. There's a story attached to it."

Each time Pam holds an object, she might pick up a different "movie" of a different person who owned the object, discovering more of the item's back story in the process.

"Objects are coveted by people," she said. "The strongest emotion they had in relation to the object is what I pick up on. It doesn't matter if 20 people have owned that object since; if someone carried it around with them everywhere they went, that is what I'll pick up on. It doesn't matter if she was the fourth person out of 20 who owned it, that's what comes through."

This was especially true of one experience illustrating the awesome power of psychometry. Pam's friend, Emily (not her real name), invited Pam and her partner in paranormal investigation, Andrew Lake, to help her understand the hauntings in her Massachusetts home. The friend was upset because her young son was having a difficult time dealing with the ghostly activity.

During the course of the investigation, Emily handed Pam a gold bracelet that her boyfriend had given to her.

"Rings and other jewelry usually have something happening, gold rings in particular," Pam said. "Gold (which is known for its electrical conductive properties) holds on to energy the best out of any metal that I've every touched."

Emily said that every time she wore the bracelet, she felt awful and didn't know why. Knowing Pam practiced psychometry, Emily wanted to know if Pam picked up anything from the bracelet.

Pam held the bracelet and closed her eyes. Her consciousness was transported to a lake.

"I could see the man the bracelet had belonged to, and then I was seeing the scene through his eyes," Pam said. "He took me into the boat with his two friends with whom he was fishing on the lake. Then suddenly, the boat tipped over and it was as if I was actually being pulled under the water myself, drowning, feeling my feet stuck in the muck at the bottom of the lake and unable to get free. I could look above me and see his friends trying to get to him, but they were too late."

As she was viewing this, Pam began to feel as if she, too, were drowning. She began thrashing around, having difficulty breathing. After the vision ended, she explained to her bewildered friend and fellow investigator what she saw.

Emily called her boyfriend to find out where he had gotten the bracelet.

"He told me it had come from his friend, Ken, and that he had drowned in a fishing accident," Pam said. "He essentially described for me the entire ordeal, and it was exactly as I'd seen it."

Pam also received a message from Ken while holding the bracelet; he was worried about his son, who had developed a drug problem. Ken told Pam that he intended to stick around to keep an eye on his son.

"Sometimes I get just a few images when holding an object, but sometimes I get whole stories. That was one of the most vivid experiences I ever had," she said.

Another time, Pam was in a marketplace and picked up a pretty necklace. As soon as she did, she was hit by the image of a horse-draw carriage riding by a streetlamp with snow on the ground.

"Although I don't know how I knew this, I felt it was someplace in Europe," she said. "I could see a girl of about 14 or 15 with a long dress on, wearing the necklace. I asked the man selling it if he knew anything about it, and he reiterated back to me everything I had seen."

While the ability to utilize psychometry gives her a different perspective on many items, it's not always a good idea to get the complete story behind every object she encounters. Pam goes through a special procedure in her mind, allowing her to turn her

When she visits antiques shops, Pam's ability helps her not only find out if the item is authentic, but also if anything is attached to it.

"I can't always depend on what I see. Something nonhuman or alien can change their appearance to make you think they're something human when they're not."

psychometric abilities on and off as she needs them so that she's not inundated with visions while perusing a flea market or yard sale, for example.

But she said it can also be quite a tool when she wants to get the entire story behind what she is buying.

"When I go to antique shops, I keep it on," she said. "If I'm buying an antique, I want to know if it's the real thing, but I also want to know if it has anything attached to it that I might not want to take home. That might be considered cheating, but I want to know."

Pam once bought a curio cabinet that she said had "a low energy" in the shop. But after she brought it home, something "not of this world" was attached to it.

"I can't always depend on what I see," she said. "Something nonhuman or alien can change their appearance to make you think they're something human when they're not, but they give off a different vibration. Humans have a certain sense to me, and these nonhuman entities are totally different."

Through a process of spiritual cleansing, she was able to remove the entity from the cabinet, which is still in her home. She said most times there's no need to remove entities attached to objects, but it can be done if needed.

Skeptics question the validity of psychometry, but Pam is able to unveil such in-depth history of objects she merely holds in her hands that those same skeptics are left scratching their heads. Paranormal investigator Matt Moniz even tried to trick Pam while at a paranormal conference. He had several examples of evidence laid out on a table, including such items as soil samples from UFO landing sites and casts of alleged Bigfoot prints. Also on the table was an ordinary brick. Matt asked Pam if she could pinpoint where the brick came from.

Pam barely had to touch the brick before she was able to pinpoint that it had come from the basement of the haunted Lizzie Borden Bed & Breakfast in Fall River, Massachusetts.

"I was floored when she said it," Matt said, something that hasn't happened often in his 25-plus years of investigating the unusual. "That's when I knew psychometry and Pam's abilities were the real deal."

Haunted Collections

Considering the awesome power of some of the haunted, possessed, and cursed items we've shared with you in these pages, you may be shocked to discover that there are a number of individuals who collect these objects. Some of them even keep them in their own homes and invite the spirits that are attached to them to make themselves known.

Paranormal investigators like Ron Kolek of the New England Ghost Project, Thomas D'Agostino of the Paranormal United Research Society, and the members of the D.C. Metro Area Ghost Watchers have acquired numerous haunted items through their years of investigation, and utilize them to conduct experiments and train new investigators on the concepts of dealing with spirits attached to objects. But there are also a few collectors out there who display their objects to the public.

Eminent paranormal researcher John Zaffis.

The most famous is the John Zaffis Museum of the Paranormal located next to Zaffis' home in Stratford, Connecticut. Zaffis, star of the Syfy channel program, *Haunted Collector*, has spent more than 35 years investigating cases of alleged haunted, possessed, or cursed objects, many of which have ended up back at his home. He began his career working with his famous aunt and uncle, legendary investigators and demonologists Ed and Lorraine Warren of the New England Society for Psychic Research (NESPR), and has become one of the most respected paranormal authorities in his own right.

Although Zaffis has clergy members conduct "binding rituals" to the objects to keep the spirits from causing further problems, many of the items are still subject to spirit activity. When a client asks Zaffis and his organization, the Paranormal Research Society of New England, to remove a haunted object, if Zaffis feels it is too powerful to remain in his museum or if the binding rituals are not enough to hinder the spirits, Zaffis will either bury the object or throw it in a body of water to eliminate its power.

Although duties with his television show have contributed to a temporary hiatus at the museum, Zaffis continues to add objects on a nearly daily basis. Many of them are featured on the website, johnzaffisparanormalmuseum.com. A clown doll, a ventriloquist's dummy, and a possible human skull used in dark rituals are some of the highlights of the Zaffis Museum. Idols, dolls, and other items associated with black magic help create a feeling of foreboding to those who enter the museum.

Long before Zaffis started his museum, his aunt and uncle displayed their collection of haunted and cursed items at their home in Monroe, Connecticut. Now run with the help of NESPR director Tony Spera, the Warrens Occult Museum is featured in NESPR's "Warrenology" events, which include lectures by Lorraine Warren and Spera and tours of the museum.

There, visitors can see items such as a satanic idol found in the Connecticut woods, an organ that plays mysteriously on its own, shrunken heads, possessed toys, and masks used for demonic projection. But the highlight of the Warrens Occult Museum is the world-famous Annabelle the Doll, as featured in the Warrens' book, *The Demonologist*.

Annabelle, a Raggedy Ann doll, was a gift to a college student in 1970. It soon began to move around on its own, even leaving creepy notes around the house. A medium told the doll's owner that it was possessed by the spirit of a seven-year-old girl, who died not far from the home, but it turned out to be something much more sinister. Annabelle was later responsible for choking and clawing a man across his chest and may even be responsible for killing another person who came in contact with it. Attempts by the Warrens and an Episcopal priest to exorcise the demonic spirits that inhabit the doll have lessened some of the power, but the doll is still known to move around on its own.

In addition to the Zaffis and Warren museums, there are other museums that warrant a visit as well. While most of them are more dedicated to paranormal investigation or strange phenomena rather than as a depository for haunted items, many do have one or two special displays of haunted objects.

The Museum of the Paranormal (museumoftheparanormal.ca), located in Niagara-on-the-Lake in Ontario, Canada, is the home of such haunted items as the Gettysburg Doll, the Post-Mortem Doll, and the Custom House boots. The most famous item there is Lizzie the Doll, whose eyes follow visitors as they move about the museum.

The Paranormal Museum in Asbury Park, New Jersey (theparanormalmuseumnj.com) has numerous exhibits at any given time, often featuring allegedly haunted objects. In addition, the museum offers ghost tours of other noted haunted locations across Asbury Park.

The International Museum of Spiritual Investigations (museumofspirits.com) is located in historically haunted Gettysburg, Pennsylvania, and operates out of a Civil War-era home. Its "Residual Room" features many allegedly haunted objects from dolls to Ouija boards. It is affordable to visit; adult admission is $2.

These are just a few sites in which the paranormal is the direct focus of the museum; there are countless other allegedly haunted objects that rest in various historical museums across the country and the world. Haunted items can be used as a hook to bring in visitors. It's like the motto we often use on "Spooky Southcoast" and at some of the events we conduct at historic locations: Come for the ghosts, stay for the history.

The high overhead cost of running a brick-and-mortar museum has led to the current trend of online museums. There are many of these on the Web, usually featuring

the private collections of investigators and other purveyors of paranormal trinkets.

Although online museums take away the ability to be in the presence of haunted objects and to feel the energy they emit, they require no travel, no admission fees, and best of all, no chance of bringing an unwanted spirit home with you!

These are just some of the hundreds of haunted items at the John Zaffis Paranormal Museum.

I Bought My
Ghost on eBay!

When the auction website eBay first hit the Internet in 1995, it became a collector's dream. Years spent painstakingly researching and locating desired items now took minutes instead, with just the click of a mouse. Tiffany glass, a rare Matchbox car, or original cigarette lighter for a 1972 Dodge Dart—it all had value to someone, somewhere and eBay allowed millions to turn unwanted items into cash.

It didn't take long before objects for sale on eBay started to be described as "haunted." Often filled with elaborate back stories and unverifiable claims, the item descriptions were intended to overinflate the value of otherwise mundane items. Although eBay has rules about selling a ghost or a spirit online, because delivery cannot be confirmed, haunted objects circumvent those rules. The item is real, even if the ghosts alleged to be attached to it are not.

Haunted objects sold on eBay are often met with skepticism by bidders, partly because of our suspicious nature regarding paranormal activity and partly because of our general distrust of the item descriptions on the auction site. One only needs to look at an eBay seller's rating and the comments listed to realize that not everyone is going to be pleased, no matter how accurate and truthful a seller tries to be. Because of the fickle nature of paranormal activity, an item may wreak havoc in one person's house, but might be dormant in another. Sometimes the auction item is not the cause of the ghostly activity—the location may already be haunted and the item simply serves as a trigger object.

Just as there's a lot to be gained by calling an eBay sale item "haunted," there's a lot of risk involved for the seller as well. If no activity manifests once the new owner has received the item, there's a good chance the seller could be hit with some negative feedback, thus devaluing him and his wares in the eyes of potential bidders.

But for the most part, haunted items on eBay are simply a sales pitch. If a person is attempting to sell a painting, for example, and numerous other prints of the same painting are for sale—well, conjure up a little ghost story and it makes your print different from all the others. There are probably hundreds of Ouija boards up for bid at any given time, with most probably selling for less than $20. But if it's a haunted Ouija board with an interesting story of dark spirit activity surrounding it—say, predicting a murder or casting a demonic spell—its value can be 10 times as much. Whether the story is true or not, the object becomes sexier to those who want it, and desirous to those who collect haunted objects.

Sociologists and psychologists often say ghost hunting is fueled by the desire to experience the adrenaline rush of fear, no different from enjoying a good horror film. Seeing an allegedly haunted object every day, with the potential for spirit activity to occur because of it, serves as a way to experience that same adrenaline rush.

Dolls, old toys, and even musical instruments lend themselves to ghost stories and tales of paranormal phenomenon. There are many reasons why. Dolls can have an inherent creepiness, but they also can be beloved and, therefore, easily subjected to spirit attachment. The same goes for a toy that was played with for many hours, or an instrument that a person spent a good portion of their lives attempting to master. The energy that was expended loving, playing with, or despising some of these objects can ingrain itself within them.

A good ghost story has also helped turn inexpensive costume jewelry and inconsequential rings into big-money items. Even if it's not gold, it can still be a goldmine.

Haunted objects sold on eBay have fetched some astounding sums. Some of the most famous have been purchased by online casino, GoldenPalace. com, which went on a bit of a spending spree for haunted items in the middle

Many items for sale on eBay are purported to be haunted or to have a spell attached to them. This 5-inch "demon" came loaded and ready for the buyer to use it for black-magic spells to smite enemies, along with a warning to "use at your own risk...not a toy!" When the buyer flipped open the box it came in, she was secretly expecting the same result as opening Pandora's Box, or perhaps the Indiana Jones version of the Ark of the Covenant. But nothing. Not even so much as a demonic burp.

Because of the fickle nature of paranormal activity, an item may wreak havoc in one person's house, but might be dormant in another. Sometimes the auction item is not the cause of the ghostly activity - the location may already be haunted and the item simply serves as a trigger object.

of the first decade of the 21st century. A grilled cheese sandwich that reportedly bore an image of the Virgin Mary was purchased in 2004 for an eye-popping $28,000. The sandwich was already 10 years old at the time and had never grown a spot of mold, so it was believed to possess some sort of supernatural power.

Later that same year, GoldenPalace.com paid $65,000 for a haunted cane that had attached to it the spirit of the old man who had used it for many years. The man's daughter put the cane up for auction because her father's spirit was allegedly disturbing her young son, and she hoped selling the cane would convince the boy that his grandfather's spirit had gone with it.

The purchase of the haunted objects was a win-win-win for all three parties involved: the seller, the buyer, and eBay. The sellers each made tidy sums for items that were otherwise of little value. GoldenPalace.com made headlines and drew attention to its site, gaining even more exposure when it took the items on a nationwide tour. And well beyond the nice eBay seller fees that came as a result of such large winning bids, eBay itself enjoyed great exposure and attention, and likely an increase in site traffic as well. It's safe to say eBay would rather see a "haunted" cane sell for $65,000 than a non-haunted one sell for $6.50.

While we are not aware of any comprehensive studies of the sale of haunted items on eBay, there *are* trends that an observer can identify. Not surprisingly, those trends also mirror the hot paranormal topic of the time. Early haunted items were said to contain average, run-of-the-mill spirits—perhaps ghosts of the former owners. As negative spirits and demons made television shows like *Paranormal State* and *Ghost Adventures* more intriguing to viewers, they also began to be attributed to haunted eBay items. The current trend as of this writing is the concept of *djinn* or *jinn*—a supernatural entity of Arabian folklore from which the word "genie" is derived—attached to items like rings and pendants. Many of these objects are said to possess a spirit that will increase your luck and make your dreams come true, as opposed to simply haunting your home.

Just as with anything purchased on eBay, a haunted object is not guaranteed to be everything claimed in the item description. You must take these descriptions with a grain of salt. Whether the items are haunted or not, the old adage remains true: buyer beware.

Photo Credits

The photographs in this book are courtesy/copyright of the following people:

P. 4-5: Michael Bednarek/Shutterstock.

P. 9: Christopher Balzano.

P. 11: Sergio Schnitzler/Shutterstock.

P. 12: Gyorgy Barna/Shutterstock.

P. 13: FomaA/Shutterstock.

P. 14: Christopher Balzano.

P. 15-16: Annette Shaff/Shutterstock.

P. 18 and 19: Dave Francis.

P. 20: Jetrel/Shutterstock.

P. 24 and 26: Dodie Claar.

P. 30: Christopher Balzano.

P. 33: Christopher Balzano.

P. 35: Christopher Balzano.

P. 36-37: Shmel/Shutterstock.

P. 39, 41 and 43: Used by permission.

P. 44: criben/Shutterstock.

P. 46: Anthony Smith/Shutterstock.

P. 49: Stephen Coburn/Shutterstock.

P. 50 and 51: Wikimedia Commons.

P. 53: Leo Balzano.

P. 56: Christopher Balzano.

P. 59: MrSegui/Shutterstock.

P. 60 and 61: Mel Slater.

P. 66-67: Guy Shapira/Shutterstock.

P. 69 and 71: Nancy Planeta.

P. 76: Poprugin Aleksey/Shutterstock.

P. 81 and 83: Christopher Balzano.

P. 85: Péter Gudella/Shutterstock.

P. 86: Wikimedia Commons.

P. 87: Wikimedia Commons.

P. 91: Jackie Barrett.

P. 92: Seulatr/Wikimedia Commons.

P. 94-95: Jeff Thrower/Shutterstock.

P. 97: Mikhail/Shutterstock.

P. 99: Valeriy Lebedev/Shutterstock.

P. 101, 102, 103, 105, 106-107, 108, 109: Christopher Balzano.

P. 111 and 113: Jill Cole.

P. 112: Stephanie Connell/Shutterstock.

P. 114: Anita Patterson Peppers/Shutterstock.

P. 118-119: Frank Grace.

P. 120 and 121: nutech21/Shutterstock.

P. 124: alison1414/Shutterstock.

P. 126-127: VitalyRomanovich/Shutterstock.

P. 128: srdjan draskovic/Shutterstock.

P. 132 and 133: John Brightman.

P. 135: Olivier Le Queinec/Shutterstock.

P. 137: Used by permission.

P. 140-141: Leigh Prather/Shutterstock.

P. 142: Everett Johnson Jr.

P. 145: Pete Donofrio/Shutterstock.

P. 149 and 151: Ray Jay Edwards.

P. 150: Pierre David/Live Entertainment.

P. 152: afitz/Shutterstock.

P. 156-157 and 159: Slava Gerj/Shutterstock.

P. 162: TriStar Pictures.

P. 165: Heritage Auctions.

P. 168 and 169: Jeannette Osbourne.

P. 178: Heritage Auctions

P. 180-181: Dmitrijs Bindemanis/ Shutterstock.

P. 183: Anastasios Kandris/ Shutterstock.

P. 186: Image Tex/Heritage Auctions.

P. 188: Mediamix photo/Shutterstock.

P. 190: Syfy television channel.

P. 192 and 193: J.W. Ocker, www.oddthingsiveseen.com; author of *The New England Grimpendium*.

P. 195: Stacey L. Brooks.

Glossary

Apparition: The visual appearance of any spirit or unusual phenomenon that doesn't necessarily take on the shape of a human form or that doesn't show signs of intelligence or personality.

Apportation: A phenomenon in which objects mysteriously appear or disappear through the influence of spirits.

Binding ritual: A form of restraint to keep a spirit attached to a certain object from causing further problems.

Demon: One of any nonhuman spirits whose objective is to possess a human.

Demonologist: Someone who studies demons and is well versed in nonhuman activity.

Djinn or jinn: A spirit often capable of assuming human or animal form and exercising supernatural influence over people. Some are helpful and can be called on to help in times of need; others are malicious demon-like creatures that cause great suffering when summoned.

Doppelganger: The spirit of a person who is living and viewed by that same person. A doppelganger is often the vision of one's own death.

Electromagnetic field (EMF): Natural and unnatural fluctuations in the magnetic fields in an area. This field can be measured, and high readings often indicate the presence of a ghost.

Electronic voice phenomenon (EVP): The noises and voices that are recorded on traditional audiotape or videotape, but aren't audible to the human ear while being recorded; often believed to be voices from the other side.

Elementals: Spirits created by forces in nature, rather than the remnants of real people.

Ghost: A visual manifestation of a soul, spirit, life force, or life energy. Most people use this term to describe the visual appearance of a human being or creature that has died and passed on to the other side.

Ghost hunter: A person who investigates and studies ghosts, hauntings, and paranormal phenomenon.

Intellectual haunting: Refers to a ghost with a mind that is still active and a "body" that can interact with the environment.

Medium: A person who has a special gift and believes he or she can act as a bridge between the world of the living and the other side.

Old hag syndrome: the feeling that some unseen force is pushing down on your chest.

Orb: A phenomenon in the shape of a floating ball of light, often thought to be a trapped soul.

Other side: The spirit world, or the place spirits go after death.

Ouija or spirit board: A flat board marked with the letters of the alphabet, the numbers 0-9, the words "yes," "no," "hello," and "goodbye," and various symbols and graphics. Thought by many to be a portal into the spirit world to allow communication, and some claim they invite darker forces like demons into the real world.

Paranormal: Unusual activity that lies outside the range of normal experience and involves ghosts, apparitions, spirits, hauntings, or poltergeists; anything for which there is no scientific explanation.

Phenomenon: A paranormal occurrence that cannot be explained in scientific terms.

Poltergeist: A mischievous spirit energy that exists solely to plague people. A newer theory is that they are caused through unconscious mental abilities manifesting in a prepubescent child.

Psychic: A person who uses empathetic feelings to tap into non-physical forces.

Psychometry: A type of extra sensory perception in which touching and holding an object can reveal its history through psychic means.

Residual haunting: A spirit that is trapped in a continuous emotional loop.

Séance: A gathering of people to receive messages from the spirit world; often conducted by a medium or psychic.

Shadow people: supernatural, shadow-like figures that can be seen flickering on walls and ceilings.

Spirit: An electromagnetic entity in the form of an orb, mist, vortex, or shadow that is the signature of a once-living person who has returned to a specific location.

Spirit attachment: The ability of a spirit to imprint energy on people, places, or things.

Spirit world: The place spirits go after death.

Supernatural: Anything beyond the accepted definitions of the natural world. Something supernatural is not necessarily ghostly.

Trigger object: A physical item, music, language or dialect used to communicate with a spirit.

Urban legend: Any story told as having happened to a friend of a friend. Many reported hauntings are recycled urban legends.

Online Resources

The following websites are just a sampling of the many you can find online that are useful resources if you want to discover more about the various aspects of paranormal activity or read more ghost stories. You can also make a specific search for any groups in your state. Keep in mind that the opinions and theories expressed on these sites are those of the individual or groups who created the site and aren't necessarily based on scientific evidence.

The Atlantic Paranormal Society
www.the-atlantic-paranormal-society.com
The Atlantic Paranormal Society (TAPS) was founded in 1990 by Jason Hawes and Grant Wilson, of the Syfy TV show *Ghost Hunters*, with the sole purpose of helping those experiencing paranormal activity by investigating its claims in a professional and confidential matter using the latest in paranormal research equipment and techniques. TAPS brings decades of experience in investigating with its pioneering equipment and techniques that has changed the field of paranormal investigating.

Ghost Village.com
www.ghostvillage.com
This is the best and most complete site on the Internet for people interested in the paranormal. Ghostvillage.com is dedicated to providing ghost research, evidence, and discussion from around the world. The site welcomes and explores all viewpoints, from the skeptical to the religious, and from the scientific to the metaphysical. It is also the main site for Jeff Belanger, one of the leading authors in the paranormal field and his

books can be purchased on the site. *Haunted Objects* author Christopher Balzano runs the paranormal news here.

Ghosts of the Prairie
www.prairieghosts.com
Troy Taylor lives in Decatur, Illinois and is the founder of the American Ghost Society. He is the author of more than 80 books on hauntings and unexplained phenomena. The American Ghost Society is a national network of ghost hunters and psychical researchers who conduct investigations into the paranormal in a non-metaphysical manner. One of its main goals is to seek out allegedly haunted locations and to assist those who are experiencing problems with the paranormal.

Also at the website is a haunted museum, a collection of exhibits on the history of the supernatural, spiritualism and ghost research. Just a few of these objects include: a haunted tintype photograph from the Civil War, a brick from the infamous St. Valentine's Day Massacre, and a haunted doll said to bring death to those who own it.

Haunted Places Directory
www.haunted-places.com
This website is a directory of haunted sites around the world and is devoted to tracking current paranormal activity and investigations. There are three main components to the site: current paranormal activity, where you can submit a case or search your area; investigations and support, if you need help or want to be certified as an investigator; and resources and research, where you can find more resources or order books or equipment.

International Ghost Hunters Society
www.ghostweb.com

This a large site with thousands of members and photographs. The site features an online store where you can buy videos, books, and pamphlets. You need to be a member to view most of the photographs, but there are many free features on the site such as a catalog of Electronic Voice Phenomena (EVP) and ghost tales.

Massachusetts Paranormal Crossroads
www.masscrossroads.com

Haunted Objects author Christopher Balzano is the founder and director of Massachusetts Paranormal Crossroads, an online collection of legends and ghost stories from Massachusetts and the surrounding states.

New England Society
for Psychic Research
www.warrens.net

The New England Society for Psychic Research was founded in 1952 by Ed and Lorraine Warren, who are considered America's preeminent experts on spirits and demonology. The society is dedicated to researching and investigating paranormal activities and its website offers summaries of investigations, photographs of the paranormal, and links to additional information. The society also offers membership and the site can be used as a reference for investigations in Connecticut and other states.

The Paranormal Network
mindreader.com

This is the website of famous paranormal investigator Loyd Auerbach. The site includes information about Auerbach's work with the paranormal, the Office of Paranormal Investigations, and links to additional information.

The Paranormal Society
www.theparanormalsociety.org

The Paranormal Society, wholly owned by Mystic Media Group, is a paranormal social networking community and media site designed to bring together those interested in the paranormal. It is the largest online paranormal social network, with a community of more than 8,000 members. At the site, you can watch paranormal shows, all fully licensed. The social community network includes personal photo and video galleries, public and private groups, events, friend system, profile wall posts, status updates, comments and more.

Paranormal X
paranormalx.net

This website is dedicated to all aspects of the paranormal. The strangest of the stories from around the internet and elsewhere make their way to the paranormal network. This site is for entertainment only and should be viewed as such.

The Shadowlands
theshadowlands.net

Since 1994, The Shadowlands has been dedicated to informing and enlightening visitors on such topics as ghosts and hauntings, mysterious creatures including Bigfoot and sea serpents, UFOs and aliens, and many other unsolved mysteries. More than 16,700 real ghost experiences have also been shared at the site by visitors.

Spooky Southcoast
www.spookysouthcoast.com

SpookySouthcoast.com is the home of one of the world's top-rated paranormal talk shows. Delve into the world of the strange and unusual each week with *Haunted Objects* author Tim Weisberg, who is the host, and "The Silent Assassin" Matt Costa, Science Adviser Matt Moniz and Content Director Chris Balzano. Ghosts, hauntings, UFOs, alien beings, cryptid creatures... nothing is too taboo with the Spooky Crew.

Index

Alexander, 32
Alves, Alan, 80, 82, 83
Amadio, Bruno, 175
American Book Company, 70
American Haunting, An, 161
Amethyst, 152
Amityville House, 90, 92
Amityville murders, 86, 90-93
Anawan, 33
Angels, 144
Annabelle the Doll, 191
Antiques shop, 28, 29, 188, 189
Apparition, 18
Apportation, 184
Arabian Nights, The, 149
Arthurian legend, 70, 72
Ashland Historical Society, 19
Assonet Ledge, 60
Atlantic Paranormal Society, The (TAPS), 68
Attachment theory, 182-184
Austrian-Hungarian Empire, 62
Awety, Daniel, 138

Bad luck, 60, 150, 151, 158, 160
Baker, Anna, 23
Baker, Elias, 23
Baker Mansion, 23
Barker, Clive, 161
Barrett, Jackie, 86-93
Barris, George, 62
Beatles, 55
Bed, 129
Belcourt Castle, 139
Bell, Elizabeth, 23
Bell Witch, 161
Belmont, Oliver Hazard Perry, 139
Bigfoot, 30, 189
Binding ritual, 190

Birth certificate, 73-79
Black magic, 132, 190
Blair County Historical Society, 23
"Bloody Mary," 138, 161, 162
Book, 13, 68-72, 89
Borden, Abby, 86
Borden, Andrew, 86
Borden, Lizzie, 86, 89
Bosnia, 63
Boston and Albany Railroad, 21
Bowlby, John, 182
Bradford, David, 162
Bridgewater Triangle, 30, 31, 33, 34, 81, 84
Brightman, John, 130, 132, 133
British Museum, 50, 51
"Broken Melody, The," 96, 98
Buchanan, Joseph Rodes, 185
Busby Stoop Chair, 138-139
Busby Stoop, Inn, 138
Busby, Thomas, 138
Butter dish, 14, 136-137

Cahill, Robert Ellis, 96
Camera, 38-43
Candyman, 161-162
Cane, 196
Cars, 60-65
Casey, David, 104
Chairs, 48, 49, 138-139
Charlesgate Hotel, 117
Charlie Daniels Band, The, 99
Children, 24
Christine, 62
Christmas angels, 58-59
Christmas ornaments, 57-58
Church, General Benjamin, 32
Claire the Doll, 110-115
Clift, Montgomery, 164
Clock, 13, 134

Clothing and accessories, 17-35
Computers, 85, 93, 150
Crying Boy, The, 175-176
Cudworth, Harold Gordon, 96, 98
Curses, 30, 50, 51, 60, 92, 100, 133, 138, 160

D'Agostino, Arlene, 177-178
D'Agostino, Thomas, 177-178, 190
Dark figures, 24, 93, 118, 121
Dark forces, 12, 84, 87, 90, 91, 92, 116, 194
*Dark Woods: Cults, Crimes, and the Para-
    normal in the Freetown State Forest, Mas-
    sachusetts*, 80, 83, 84
D.C. Metro Area Ghost Watchers, 190
Dean, James, 61, 62
DeFeo, Ronald Jr., 86, 90, 91, 92, 93
del Gesu, Guarneri, 96
Dell, Jeremy Wade, 179
Demonologist, 168, 171, 190
Demonologist, The, 191
Demons, 12, 149, 191, 195, 196
Devil, 99, 158
*Devil I Know: My Haunting Journey with
    Ronnie DeFeo and the True Story of the
    Amityville Murders, The*, 93
"Devil Went Down to Georgia, The," 99
"Devil's Trill Sonata," 98, 99
Djinn/jinn, 148-151, 196
Dolls, 10, 11, 13, 15, 100-115, 131, 133, 174,
    184, 190, 191, 195
Doppelgangers, 12
Dresses, 18-23, 24, 25, 26, 27

East Martello Museum, 102
Eastern Airlines, 64, 65
eBay, 148, 149, 174, 175, 194-196
Eckles, Damon, 86
Eclectic Medical Institute, 185
Egypt, 50, 51
Egyptian artifacts, 50
Electrical devices, ghost communication
    and, 10
Electronic voice phenomena (EVP), 70-71,
    115, 149, 151
Elementals, 12

EMF detector/meter, 104, 114, 149, 151
Eschrid, William, 62
Excalibur, 70

Fairbanks, Douglas, 164
Ferdinand, Archduke Franz, 62, 63
File cabinet, 73, , 74, 78
Flight 401, 64-65
Flight Safety Foundation, 65
Folklore, 8
Forbidden, The, 161
Fournier, Leonard "Cappy," 18
Francis, David, 19, 21, 22
Freetown, Massachusetts, 80, 82, 83
Freetown State Forest, 33, 34
From Here to Eternity, 164
Fuller, John, 65

Generation X, 178
Gentlemen Prefer Blondes, 165
Gettysburg Doll, 191
Ghost Adventures, 196
Ghost hunters, 8, 82
Ghost Hunters, 68
Ghost Hunters television show, 19, 162
Ghost of Flight 401, The, 65
Ghost stories, 8, 100, 110, 174, 194, 195
Ghost tones, 99
Ghosts, 8, 10, 12, 13, 14, 15, 18, 22, 24, 31,
    33, 34, 42, 46, 47, 49, 54, 60, 64, 68, 77,
    78, 79, 80, 87, 88, 98, 125, 139, 144, 146,
    147, 163, 187, 194
Ghosts I Have Known, 96
Glasses, 14
Gold bracelet, 187
Gold rings, 187
Golden Palace, 195-196
Gräf & Stift Bois de Boulogne tourer, 62-64
Graves and Gravestones, 101, 104
Grilled cheese sandwich, 196
Guinness, Alex, 61

Haitian masks, 168-173
Hands Resist Him, The, 174-175
Harnois, Brian, 19

Haunted collections, 190-193
Haunted Collector, 190
Haunted Violin: True New England Ghost Stories, The, 96
Hawthorne, Nathaniel, 30
Heirlooms, 13, 38
Heeresgeschichtliches Museum, 63
Hollywood Roosevelt Hotel, 164-165
Holmes, Dr. H.H., 86
Hornsteiner, Joseph, 96, 98
House That Kay Built, The, 89
Household items, 14, 15

Ilmu Khodam, 149
Intelligent haunting, 10, 68
International Museum of Spiritual Investigations, The, 191

Jack the Ripper, 86
"Jeremy," 179
Jewelry, 140-155,195
John Zaffis Museum of the Paranormal, 133, 171, 173, 190-191, 192

Kenobi, Obi-Wan, 61
Kolek, Ron, 190
King Arthur, 70
King, Stephen, 30, 62
King Philip's War, 32, 34

Lady of the Lake, The, 68-72
Lake, Andrew, 187
Lalande, Jerome, 99
Lamps, 12
Ledger, Heath, 62
Legends, 23, 38, 50, 61, 98, 99, 161
Lilith's Cave: Jewish Tales of the Supernatural, 98
Linda White Antique Clothing, 21
Little Bastard, 61, 62
Lizzie Borden Bed and Breakfast, 13, 86-90, 93, 189
Lizzie the Doll, 191
Lodi, Edward, 96, 98
Loft, Bob, 64

"Lord's Prayer," 81-83
Lovecraft, H.P., 30
Lutz family, 90

Macumba, 132, 133
Magic, 100
Man Who Shot Liberty Valance, The, 23
Marble, 144-147
Marley, John, 174
Massasoit, 32
Mayer, Louis B., 164
McHenry, Troy, 62
Mediums, 34, 132, 185, 191
Merlin, 70
Mirror legends, 161-162
Mirror superstitions, 159-160
Mirrors, 158-165
Moniz, Matt, 84, 189
Monroe, Marilyn, 164-165
Museum of the Paranormal, The, 191
Mummy, 50-51
Music box, 112, 113
Myers, Frances, 164
Myers, James, 164
Myrtles Plantation, 162-164
"Mysterious New England," 96
Myths, 50

Necklace, 47
New England Ghost Project, 190
New England Paranormal Research, 130, 132
New England Society for Psychic Research, 190, 191
New England's Ghostly Haunts, 96
Night of the Living Dead, 177-178
Norris, Curt, 96, 98

"Object recognition," 185
Old hag syndrome, 45
Old Scratch, 99
Otto, Robert Eugene, 100, 101
Otto, Robert Eugene Jr., 100, 101
Ouija and spirit boards, 116-125, 191, 194

Paintings, 8, 174-176
Paranormal activity, 8, 12, 13, 14, 19, 34, 35, 60, 71, 82, 84, 86, 88, 109, 110, 120, 122, 130, 144, 150, 151, 166, 169, 170, 171, 172, 173, 175, 184, 194
Paranormal investigators/researchers, 19, 58, 65, 68. 84, 130, 133, 148-151, 168, 171, 172, 177, 182, 187, 189, 190
Paranormal Museum, The, 191
Paranormal Research Society of New England, 190
Paranormal State, 196
Paranormal United Research Society, 190
Parasol, 28-29
Pareidolia, 164
Patalano, Pam, 185-189
Pearl Jam, 179
Philip, 32
Photographs/pictures, 13, 38, 41, 54, 55, 82, 83, 166-167
Pickford, Mary, 164
Pilgrims, 31, 32
Pink flamingo, 48, 49
Planeta, Nancy, 65, 68-72
Plates, 14
Plymouth Colony, 32
Plymouth Rock, 30
Poltergeist, 100
Poltergeists, 12, 171
Post-Mortem Doll, 191
Posters, 177-179
Potiorek, General Oskar, 63
Porche 550 Spyder, 61, 62
Presley, Elvis, 62
Princess of Amen-Ra, 50
Profile Rock, 33
Psychic, 13, 86, 88, 185
Psychometer, 185
Psychometry, 185, 187, 188, 189
Pukwudgies, 31

Queen Mary I, 161

Radios, 55
Railroad House, 18

Repo, Don, 64, 65
Residual haunting, 10, 12, 185
Retalic, David, 19, 21
Richardson High School, 179
Rings, 148-151, 187
RMS *Titanic*, 51
Robert the Doll, 100-109
Robinson, Charles, 32
Romans, 158, 160

Sachem, 32
Sarcophagus, 50, 51
Saint Raphael medal, 153-155
Satan, 80
Séance, 88, 91
Schwartz, Howard, 98
Scott House, The, 68, 69, 71, 72
Scott, Maxwell, 23
Scott, Mrs. Elizabeth, 69, 70
Scott, Sir Walter, 69, 70
Sea salt, 151
Serbia, 63
Seven Sisters Inn, 68
Shadow people, 12
Shakur, Tupac, 62
Sheet music, 98
Silverware, 12
Slave Chloe, 162-164
Smith, Mary J., 18, 19, 21, 22
Spera, Tony, 191
Spirit attachment, 182-184
Spirits, 10, 12, 13, 18, 24, 38, 46, 48, 52. 54, 65, 68, 71, 78, 88, 92, 117-119, 123, 132, 133, 139, 161, 163, 164, 164, 166, 171, 182, 184, 185, 194, 196
Spiritualist movement, 185
Spiritualists, 34, 51, 185
"Spooky Southcoast," 93, 192
St. Christopher, 142
St. Christopher's medal, 142-143, 184
Stead, William Thomas, 51
Stone, Captain John, 18, 22
Stone's Public House, 18, 19, 22
Stoneham, Bill, 174
Stradivari, Antonio, 96

Sullivan, Bridget, 88
Superstition, 12
Syfy, 19, 190

Talky Tina, 100
Tartini, Giuseppe, 99
Tartinin tones, 99
Telekinetic energy, 12
Temperature, ghost and spirit presence and, 8, 57-58, 115, 125, 129, 139
Thirsk Museum, 138, 139
Thrift shop, 28
Thunderbirds, 31
Time slips, 12
Tinney family, 139
Tinney, Harle Hope Hanson, 139
Tools, 29, 52-55
Toys, 24, 195
Trapped energy, 12
Trigger object, 184, 194
Twilight Zone, The, 100

UFOs, 30,189
Underground Railroad, 18
Unsolved Mysteries, 162
Urban legend, 60-62, 179

Vampires, 158
Van Biene, Auguste, 98
Virgin Mary, 196
Violin, 96-99
"Violin Sonata in G Minor," 99
von Liebig, Justus, 158
Voodoo, 100, 131, 133
Voyage d'un Francois en Italie, 99

Wampanoag Indian Tribe, 30-35, 80
Wampum belt, 30-35
Warren, Ed, 171, 190, 191
Warren, Lorraine, 171, 190, 191
Warrens Occult Museum, 191
Watches, 13
Webster, Daniel, 8
Wedding dress, 23
West Memphis 3, 86
White, Linda, 21, 22
Witch, 8, 45, 149, 158
Woodruff, Clark, 162, 163
Woodruff, Cordelia, 162, 163
Woodruff, James, 162, 163
Woodruff, Mary, 162-163
Woodruff, Sara, 162, 163, 164
World War I, 62
World War II, 138
Worth, Mary, 161

Yankee Magazine, 96
Yard sales, 10, 15, 73, 185
Yeats, William Butler, 168
Young girl ghosts/spirits, 18, 24-26, 54, 57, 88, 89, 90
Yugoslavia, 63

Zaffis, John, 133, 171, 173, 190-191
Zombies, 31

About the Authors

Christopher Balzano is the founder and director of Massachusetts Paranormal Crossroads, an online collection of legends and ghost stories from Massachusetts and the surrounding states. He has been a contributor to Jeff Belanger's *Encyclopedia of Haunted Places* and *Weird Massachusetts* and was one of the writers behind *Weird Hauntings*. He has appeared in more than a dozen other books, often called in to offer insight into the paranormal perspective of certain cases. His writing has been featured in *Haunted Times* and *Mystery Magazine* and has been covered by *The Boston Globe*, *The Boston Herald*, *The Standard Times*, *Worcester Magazine*, and many other print and online publications.

Christopher is the author of several books about regional hauntings, including *Dark Woods: Cults, Crime, and Paranormal in the Freetown State Forest* and *Ghosts of the Bridgewater Triangle*, as well as the collection of true ghosts stories, *Ghostly Adventures*, and the how-to paranormal books, *Picture Yourself Ghost Hunting* and *Picture Yourself Capturing Ghosts on Film*.

He has appeared on radio stations in New England and Florida and throughout the Internet, as well as being called upon by television shows to comment on ghosts and urban legends, including the British television series, *Conversations with a Serial Killer*. He has been a guest on Coast to Coast AM and been asked in as a consultant on televisions shows like *Paranormal State* and *Ghost Adventures*. He now runs the paranormal news from Ghostvillage.com, one of the oldest and largest websites dedicated to the paranormal and is the content director for the popular paranormal radio show, "Spooky Southcoast."

Tim Weisberg is the host of "Spooky Southcoast," one of the world's most popular radio programs dealing with the subject of the paranormal (www.spookysouthcoast.com), and is one of the foremost authorities on the hauntings at the world-famous Lizzie Borden Bed and Breakfast in Fall River, Massachusetts.

Tim has appeared on *MonsterQuest* on the History Channel, *Ghost Adventures* and *Most Terrifying Places in America*, both on the Travel Channel, *My Ghost Story* on the BIO Channel, *LIVING TV* in the UK, and "30 Odd Minutes." He has also co-founded Legend Trips, a paranormal events company.

He has been featured in publications such as *FATE Magazine*, *SoCo Magazine* and *SouthCoast Insider*. A sportswriter by trade, Tim covers the Boston Celtics and the New England Patriots for *The Standard-Times* of New Bedford, Massachusetts. He is also the author of *Ghosts of the SouthCoast*, published by History Press.